Student Goals for College and Cour...
A Missing Link in Assessing and Improving Academic Achievement

by Joan S. Stark, Kathleen M. Shaw, and Malcolm A. Lowther

ASHE-ERIC Higher Education Report 6, 1989

Prepared by

Clearinghouse on Higher Education
The George Washington University

In cooperation with

Association for the Study
of Higher Education

Published by

School of Education and Human Development
The George Washington University

Jonathan D. Fife, Series Editor

Cite as
Stark, Joan S., Kathleen M. Shaw, and Malcolm A. Lowther. *Student Goals for College and Courses* Report No. 6. Washington, D.C.: School of Education and Human Development, The George Washington University, 1989.

Library of Congress Catalog Card Number 89-63442
ISSN 0884-0040
ISBN 0-9623882-4-6

Managing Editor: Christopher Rigaux
Manuscript Editor: Katharine Bird
Cover design by Michael David Brown, Rockville, Maryland

The ERIC Clearinghouse on Higher Education invites individuals to submit proposals for writing monographs for the *ASHE-ERIC Higher Education Report* series. Proposals must include:
1. A detailed manuscript proposal of not more than five pages.
2. A chapter-by-chapter outline.
3. A 75-word summary to be used by several review committees for the initial screening and rating of each proposal.
4. A vita and a writing sample.

ERIC Clearinghouse on Higher Education
School of Education and Human Development
The George Washington University
One Dupont Circle, Suite 630
Washington, DC 20036-1183

This publication was prepared partially with funding from the Office of Educational Research and Improvement, U.S. Department of Education, under contract no. ED RI-88-062014. The opinions expressed in this report do not necessarily reflect the positions or policies of OERI or the Department.

EXECUTIVE SUMMARY

As the United States debates what it expects of college graduates and how to measure the achievement of these expectations, the goals of students frequently are overlooked. During discussions about higher education quality, activities such as promoting active involvement in learning, stating clear expectations, and assessing educational results have taken on increased importance for colleges and universities attempting to improve their programs. Yet in each of these activities, understanding students' educational goals is important to ensure success. Helping students take active responsibility for their education, for example, may depend on how well educators link the classroom goals they set for their students with the goals that students hold for themselves. Communicating clear expectations for students depends, in part, on understanding discrepancies between expectations instructors establish and those students accept as consistent with their own goals. In addition, accurate assessment of student outcomes fostered by the college experience should take into account students' educational goals as well as their academic preparation.

What Are Goals?
Goals are what individuals hope to achieve and accomplish. Such intentions motivate and direct human behavior. Thus, educational outcomes such as academic satisfaction, use of appropriate learning strategies, effort exerted in course work, and ultimately, academic achievement, are related to goals. Goals are not fixed; they change as individuals develop different self-views and acquire new methods of regulating their behavior. In fact, helping students to revise their goals and to improve the extent to which they control their behavior are valid educational goals.

**What Information About Students'
Goals Do Colleges Typically Collect?**
Currently, most colleges collect information about the broad goals students hold for attending college as they enter. This information is used for administrative planning or for developing strategies to recruit and retain students. Some institutions also collect perceptions from graduating seniors and alumni about the extent to which they achieved their academic, personal, social, and vocational goals in college. Apparently, few institutions make the effort to measure how student

goals change from entrance to graduation or as a result of specific programs of study.

In attempting to examine goals more systematically, scholars of higher education have developed a number of typologies based on observed student subcultures or broad intellectual orientations (for example, Katchadourian and Boli 1985). Researchers related these typologies to student characteristics believed to be relatively stable, such as learning styles and vocational orientations, and used them to increase understanding of problems such as student attrition. Typologies are criticized, however, for perpetuating stereotypes of students.

Since goals are what students hope to accomplish, and outcomes represent what actually is achieved, current trends toward measurement of educational outcomes (assessment) foster attempts to connect goals and outcomes at the course and program level. A few colleges, active in developing student assessment programs, also are collecting and using information about specific student goals for classroom work. Increasingly, educators and researchers recognize that the impact of college might be measured more effectively at the program or course level, close to the student's everyday educational environment. As yet, however, systematic attempts to include student goals in assessment and instructional improvement activities are limited.

Do New Concepts Hold Promise for Student Goal Data?

Although social scientists' knowledge about motivation, goals, and related ideas has progressed substantially in recent years, educators have been slow to use this knowledge in studies of student goals. Commonly used goals instruments tend to fall at either end of a continuum. At one extreme, college administrators collect data about broad college goals; at the other extreme, psychologists study the goals students set when performing specific learning tasks. Because of their breadth, statements used in institutional-level surveys of college goals, such as "I want to develop intellectually," fail to discriminate meaningfully between groups of students, even those likely to choose different majors. In addition, faculty, administrators, and policy makers often ignore as excessively technical explorations of student learning behaviors illustrated by goal statements such as "when I read an assignment, I try to relate new ideas to things I already know."

Early studies of student goals developed from a psychological orientation that still predominates. Recently, cognitive psychologists have focused on processes of self-regulation used by learners. These include setting goals, preparing cognitively for action, and establishing a cycle of self-monitoring behavior (Markus and Wurf 1987). In understanding these processes, researchers examine variables such as self-concept, motivation, and other organizing strategies used by learners.

Although not always immediately useful to classroom instructors because of complex terminology, these studies helped clarify that goals are changeable and closely linked with both self-concept and the possession of learning skills. This interdependence between self-view and learning suggests that educators should give increasing attention as well to sociological perspectives that stress cultural and social determinations of goal choice. Viewing the classroom as a specific environment where self-concept, motivation, goals, and learning behaviors all are influenced makes it obvious that faculty should build upon goals in course planning. A sociological perspective also encourages instructors to predict and observe goal change over time as a potential outcome of specific instructional strategies.

Recently, social scientists identified goal attributes such as specificity, clarity, source, commitment, and temporality. These can help to better define goals or to relate college experiences to goal attainment. In part, scientific attention to these attributes and progress toward measuring them merely makes explicit what good teachers have long known through observation. To illustrate, instructors readily recognize that a potentially excellent student is one who has established a strong commitment to a clear, long-term educational goal. When such a student fails to achieve in accord with expectations, the cause may lie not with the goal, but with one or more of its specific attributes.

Perhaps, despite apparent strong commitment, the long-term goal lacked clarity. Possibly the goal source was parental aspirations, rather than student aspirations. Perhaps the student failed to develop short-term and specific course goals gradually leading toward the intended achievement. Such consideration of goal attributes could help diagnose educational problems and help to improve learning, if suitable measurement inventories were available.

What Are the Characteristics of a
Course-Specific Student Goals Inventory?

Based on their prior preparation and self-views, students have broad goals for attending college, narrower goals for achievement in particular courses, and even more specific goals as they approach each learning task. The goals students bring to college courses are interrelated in time with the broader college goals that precede them and the narrower, specific learning task goals that help to achieve them. Ideally, then, to provide the broadest possible understanding of student goals, an inventory for classroom use would include items concerning broad goals, expectancies, and self-concept, as well as goals specific to the type of courses.

Many possible frameworks could guide development of such an inventory. For example, a framework could emphasize a single goal area, for example, goals related to intellectual growth, social and personal growth, or vocational growth. An appropriate inventory could be based, as well, on theories of intellectual development such as those established by Kolb, Perry or Bloom. New developments in social science can help to guide development of a comprehensive course-specific students goals inventory capable of illuminating the multi-dimensional goal patterns students bring to college and classroom.

A comprehensive model of student goals promises considerably more explanatory power than previous simpler goal models, and presents an extensive complex set of possibilities for research and classroom improvement.

How Can Instructors Use
Course-Specific Goal Information?

Faculty can use students' course-level goals to improve teaching. Evidence gathered from faculty indicates that many instructors are interested in student goals, and many are willing to experiment with ways to systematically collect and use goal information (Stark, Lowther, Ryan, Bomotti, Genthon, Martens, and Haven 1988).

At the simplest and most descriptive level, goal information can help an instructor understand the diversity and intensity of student effort in a particular class. In a more elaborate way, through the process now frequently referred to as "classroom research," instructors can use goal information to discern how their goals for a particular class relate to those of their students. This can help them design classes that employ teaching approaches appropriate for their students' levels of interest and expectation. At still a more complex level, collecting and analyzing student goals can enhance formal assessment processes. Since course-level goals are measured with regard to a specific academic discipline or classroom setting, using them in the assessment process may involve statistically adjusting outcome expectations in that setting to account for goals of entering students. Assessment also may include attempts to foster and document goal changes among students.

A course-level goal inventory, the Student Goals Exploration, is current being field tested at the National Center for Research to Improve Postsecondary Teaching and Learning (NCRIPTAL). This inventory will be available soon for use by classroom teachers and researchers.

ADVISORY BOARD

CONSULTING EDITORS

Trudy W. Banta
Research Professor
University of Tennessee

Leonard L. Baird
Professor of Education
University of Kentucky

Louis W. Bender
Director, State and Regional Higher Education Center
Florida State University

Larry Braskamp
Associate Vice Chancellor for Academic Affairs
University of Illinois

L. Leon Campbell
Provost and Vice President for Academic Affairs
University of Delaware

Darrell Clowes
Associate Professor of Education
Viginia Tech

Susan Cohen
Associate, Project for Collaborative Learning
Lesley College

John W. Creswell
Professor and Lilly Project Director
University of Nebraska

Andre Deruyttere
Vice President
Catholic University at Leuven, Belgium

Mary E. Dilworh
Director, Research and Information Services
ERIC Clearinghouse on Teacher Education

James A. Eison
Director, Center for Teaching and Learning
Southeast Missouri State University

Lawrence Erickson
Professor and Coordinator of Reading and Language Studies
Southern Illinois University

Yolanda T. Moses
Vice President for Academic Affairs
California State University

Michael T. Nettles
Senior Research Scientist
Educational Testing Service

Elizabeth M. Nuss
Executive Director
National Association of Student Personnel Administrators

Jeffrey H. Orleans
Executive Director
Council of Ivy Group Presidents

Wayne Otto
Professor of Curriculum and Instuction
University of Wisconsin

John E. Roueche
Professor and Director
Community College Leadership Program
Sid W. Richardson Regents Chair
University of Texas

Mary Ellen Sheridan
Director of Sponsored Programs Administration
Ohio State University

William F. Stier, Jr.
Professor and Director of Intercollegiate Athletics
State University of New York at Brockport

Betty Taylor
Dean of the Graduate School
Lesley College

Reginald Wilson
Senior Scholar
American Council on Education

CONTENTS

FOREWORD

It is an accepted truth that motivation is a key ingredient in achieving an objective. However, without careful assessment of the individual goals that help generate the motivation, the end result may be wrongly interpreted. For example, it may be the goal of a student's parents for the student to become a lawyer. However, if one of the governing values of the student is not to disappoint the parents, the achievement of receiving a law degree may be motivated by two entirely different goals. Because there is not careful assessment of the student's goal, the end result will be an individual entering a career without the motivation to succeed beyond the attainment of the degree.

The foundation of most human action is the governing values of the individual. Goal-setting is the act of assessing and operationalizing short-term and intermediate action-oriented, measurable, and time-specific accomplishments that will allow an individual to actualize their governing ideas.

As clearly pointed out in this monograph by Joan Stark, Kathleen Shaw, and Malcolm Lowther of the National Center for Research to Improve Postsecondary Teaching and Learning at the University of Michigan, there has been minimal effort to link the objectives of a class with a student's goals. By having both the professor and the student more actively aware of the inter-relationships between the purpose of the course and the goals of the student, there will be a higher motivation to achieve and greater tendencies for retention. This report provides an overview of current methodology, and makes recommendation for how data collection can be improved by linking goals to individual classes. Recent work done by social scientists on goal-setting provides important clues for faculty. The authors conclude that a comprehensive model of student goals in within reach, and suggest how instructors can best use such a device.

Life is often likened to a ship navigating the seas. The person without conscious goals resembles a ship without a compass and a destination. Faculty who purposefully relate their courses' academic objectives to individual student goals help students to continuously define their direction and build their compass.

Jonathan D. Fife
Professor and Director
ERIC Clearinghouse on Higher Education

School of Education and Human Development
The George Washington University

ACKNOWLEDGMENTS

This manuscript was prepared with support from the National Center for Research to Improve Postsecondary Teaching and Learning (NCRIPTAL) at the University of Michigan under OERI Grant No. G008690010. The opinions expressed are those of the authors.

In compiling this report we have drawn, with permission, upon unpublished academic papers completed by students at the University of Michigan. Student authors to whom we owe credit include Sally Smith Bomotti, Jean Chagnon, and Dong Ok Kim. We also gained greatly from substantive and editorial comments contributed by research assistants Gretchen Martens and Michael P. Ryan. Finally, the report would not have been completed without the diligent word processing help of our secretary Janie Knieper.

WHY MEASURE STUDENT GOALS?

As higher education in the United States opened its doors to a great diversity of students after World War II, it became apparent that students had different goals as well as a wide range of socioeconomic backgrounds, abilities, and learning styles. Since 1966, well-known researchers have assessed the goals of many entering college students annually (Astin, Green, and Korn 1987). Recently, the American press demonstrated considerable interest in their survey of entering college students' goals.

The press and the public are concerned that, when asked to rate items from a short list of college and life goals, student choices increasingly seem vocational and less frequently are altruistic or contemplative. The researchers illustrated these trends with graphs comparing student responses to two statements: "to develop a meaningful philosophy of life," and "to be very well-off financially." In 1977, financial well-being became more important than developing a meaningful philosophy. These trends have continued through 1986 (Astin, Green, and Korn 1987, p. 23).

Public attention to those findings is not misplaced. In contrast to the press, however, the higher education community seems to have neglected the important topic of student goals. There are several reasons why educators, as well as the public, should give considerable attention to the goals of college students.

By obtaining measures of student goals, institutions should be able to relate them to other student characteristics and the curriculum to improve the educational process.

What Can Student Goals Reveal?

In the simplest and most basic terms, goals are what individuals hope to achieve and accomplish. Such intentions motivate and direct human behavior. Since goals are what students hope to achieve, many educational outcomes are related to them. These outcomes include academic satisfaction, use of appropriate learning strategies, effort exerted in course work, and, ultimately, academic achievement. Indeed, according to psychologists, "the goals individuals are pursuing create the framework within which they interpret and react to events" (Dweck and Leggett 1988, p. 256). Thus, by obtaining measures of student goals, institutions should be able to relate them to other student characteristics and the curriculum to improve the educational process. It is important to note, however, that goals are not fixed; they change as individuals develop different self-views and acquire new methods of self-management. A college's mission determines which changes in goals to encourage, or discourage, among students.

In addition to that broad rationale for the importance of considering student goals, there are more specific reasons. Among them are:

Developing curricula

Since entering college students attempt to behave in ways that will enable them to achieve those goals they see as useful and valuable, understanding student goals can help educators develop curricula that promote learning by capitalizing on student goals and their accompanying motivations. While some critics of higher education have proposed making academic programs more rigorous and required, psychologists tell us that students tend to learn at their own pace and in their own style; they are more likely to process, retain, and use information that is meaningful to them.

Unless colleges have other means of persuading students to take required academic programs, educators must pay attention to the variability of student goals and the effects they have on program enrollments. Course designs that accommodate a variety of student goals can help an institution increase student motivation to learn without becoming subservient to consumer whims or educational fads.

Improving teaching

Teaching is an act of communication. If student goals are made explicit, the way an instructor arranges, presents, or describes course material has the potential to foster improved dialogue between student and teacher. However, the teacher's communications must be directed at the student for important messages to be heard and understood. The more a student communicates with a faculty member, the more likely the teacher will understand his or her audience. As a result, a course can become more satisfying to both teacher and student. The process may be facilitated if faculty members actively seek out information on student goals within the classroom.

Assessing college outcomes

Assessing the academic achievement of students and graduates cannot be done without considering what students knew before they entered college. Just as importantly, assessment also must take into account student goals. Educational goals of entering students, individually and collectively, should be important measures in assessment efforts. This is apparent particularly at community colleges, where educators have raised legitimate objections to using degree completion as a measure of success for students who enrolled with many other types of goals, including personal enrichment, short-term occupational improvement, and others. But it is no less true at other colleges where student goals affect student effort, which, in turn, affects, and even can predict, student learning.

Assessing classroom achievement

Colleges are trying new ways to assess student development using various cognitive and noncognitive measures of growth (Adelman 1988; Mentkowski and Loacker 1985). As colleges grapple with the complexities of measurement, it increasingly is apparent that student goals act as mediators between the outcomes instructors intend and those students actually achieve. College instructors legitimately resist assessment based on the fear (long ago expressed by teachers at lower educational levels) that this mediating effect will be over-looked; without adequate measures of student goals, instruc-tors teaching very different groups of students may be com-pared unjustly.

This concern about inappropriate comparisons parallels recent discussions in which institutional administrators emphasize the importance of assessing institutions according to their unique missions (Jacobi, Astin and Ayala 1987; Ross-mann and El-Khawas 1987). Making judgments of educational "success" while ignoring specific objectives, or ranking insti-tutions while ignoring their quite different missions, is unten-able. Similarly, whenever faculty efforts are likely to be com-pared, few would dispute that discipline and course objectives first must be specified. In addition, balanced comparisons will include consideration of how student preparation and student goals interact with course work to affect educational outcomes.

Assessing goal changes

Most colleges intend to modify students' goals, attitudes, and values in selected ways. It is possible to consider shifts in stu-dent goals as appropriate outcomes that are enhanced by, and attributed to, specific educational experiences. An example is the hope that by teaching students to recognize and interpret artistic works, their leisure goals will include pursuit and enjoyment of the arts. It also is important to know if goals are shifting in unexpected ways. Examples include female students' increased aversion to mathematics, or students' declining religious commitment in colleges with religious missions. Because educators desire to change goals in selected directions, measurement of both student goals and academic learning can assist in determining whether a college is meeting its objectives.

Strengthening counseling

Colleges have an obligation to help students improve goal clarity, strengthen learning strategies, and choose wisely among achievable life and career plans. Measuring students' goals upon arriving at college or entering a particular program of concentration provides a diagnostic tool and a focal point for discussion by qualified counselors and faculty members. With underprepared students, it often is necessary for counselors to assist in establishing achievable short-term goals that can boost their self-images. Even for well-prepared, self-confident students, careful advising can help them to select particular academic experiences which will aid them in achieving specific goals.

Students entering college immediately are exposed to a bewildering array of new experiences and opportunities. At the same time, educators hope students will take responsibility for fashioning a coherent learning plan which will cultivate personal and intellectual growth as well as lead to a college degree. Students do not always see the relationship between intellectual growth and obtaining educational credentials. Under such circumstances, conscious efforts to help students set goals can aid the college in creating and maintaining a supportive, reinforcing learning environment. "When plans become clearly formulated, learning becomes organized in relation to them" (Chickering 1974, p. 113).

Recruiting students

When administrators recruit new students, they should pay attention to the "fit" between the college mission and the students' goals as well as with enrolling adequate numbers. To demonstrate this concern for a good fit, colleges should describe themselves and their current students accurately so new students do not find themselves in an alien environment.

Supplying a profile of the goals and interests of students already enrolled can help to provide an accurate recruiting picture and help new students make wise institutional choices (Stark 1977).

Retaining students

Paying attention to student-environment fit at admission time can reduce attrition rates. Subsequently, when counselors and faculty members show concern about student goals and act to accommodate them, they may help students to feel important and thus increase retention. That such efforts can work is based on the related finding that students who have out-of-class contact with faculty are integrated more closely into the academic fabric of the institution (Wilson, Gaff, Dienst, Wood, and Bavry 1975). In instances where persistence in a course or at college may not be in a student's best interest, knowledge of goals can also help counselors provide useful advice about viable alternatives.

Administrative planning

Although detailed discussion of the potential uses of information about student goals for administrative planning is beyond the scope of this report, others have discussed varied administrative reasons for collecting data on student goals. These include assessing student self-perceived educational outcomes, determining the extent to which entrance goals are achieved, anticipating and planning for enrollment changes, accommodating specific demands for services, predicting staff needs, allocating resources effectively, generating required external reports, participating in financial aid programs, reviewing academic programs and student services, and communicating with legislators and other funding agencies (National Center for Higher Education Management Systems and the College Board 1983, pp. 1–11).

Achieving basic understanding

Researchers seek to understand more about human learning, motivation, interests, and achievement. Recent psychological research has advanced our understanding of these factors and the contexts in which they operate. As a result, educators can link student goals more productively than in the past to other factors known to affect college achievement. These include motivation, the extent to which an individual feels prepared or capable of achieving a goal (self-efficacy), and effort. As such links are explored, researchers must develop new and more sensitive student goal measures. New research findings may help us to better understand and improve the learning process. Since few research studies of academic achievement have included student goals in the student success equation, the potential is largely untapped. Researchers discuss this deficiency in their report of a study on student academic growth, stating:

> *While this study included as a background (and exogenous) variable students' goals with regard to the highest degree expected, the failure here to include measures of students' commitments to achieving other academic and career/vocational goals is more problematic. These commitments might well be expected to influence, for example, the amount of effort a student exerts, which, in turn, is likely to affect the level of that student's academic (and possibly social) integration* (Terenzini and Wright 1987, p. 166).

> *While the exclusion of some measure of institutional commitment probably has had little effect on the results reported, the effects of omitting measures of students' levels of commitments to a variety of educational and vocational goals are harder to estimate* (p. 175).

An Unbalanced Equation

With so many important reasons to measure student goals, one might expect educators and policymakers to emphasize student goals in recent recommendations for improving higher education. This is not the case; rather, the emphasis of recent reports has been on clarifying and assessing the institutional goals of colleges.

Perhaps the most student-oriented of the recent reports, *Involvement in Learning* (National Institute of Education Study Group 1984), called for the use of already known information about student learning and growth to improve "three critical conditions of excellence: (1) student involvement; (2) high expectations; and (3) assessment and feedback" (pp. 17–22). As part of the assessment and feedback discussion, NIE members included assessing students' "knowledge, capacities and skills" as well as the "stated objectives of undergraduate education at their institutions" (p. 57). Additionally, they speak generally of "using assessment as a teaching tool" (p. 58).

But despite potential connections between goals and "student involvement," the group placed little emphasis on student goals or the need to understand them more completely. Negative reaction to this omission surfaced at many conferences, primarily from community college educators who pointed out that their adult students may not have the same goals and needs as traditional-age college students.

Similarly, the report *Integrity in the College Curriculum* (Association of American Colleges 1985) focused heavily on recommendations to improve the college curriculum and teaching role. In discussing the issue of accountability, the AAC commission gave only brief mention to acquiring knowledge about students and using it to improve the curriculum process. In contrast to the AAC task force's emphasis on the general education needed by college students, the report *To Secure the Blessings of Liberty* stressed the important dual role colleges play in supplying highly trained specialists for the nation's economy, and providing upward mobility for all young people (American Association of State Colleges and Universities 1986). Published by an association of colleges with high percentages of career-oriented students, the report stepped considerably closer to describing student goals as they were reported nationally, but remained some distance from discussing such goals as important educational variables.

The Carnegie Foundation for the Advancement of Teaching (Boyer 1987) reported the results of its survey of students and parents about the reasons for college attendance (p. 12). A slightly higher percentage of parents than students endorsed the goal "to gain a well-rounded education," while students more often than parents favored "to have a more satisfying career." In the following discussion, Boyer related these survey results to choice among colleges but neglected their implications for the learning process. Even in an extensive discussion of the need for improved advising in colleges (pp. 51–57, 289), student goals seldom were mentioned. Drawing upon Carnegie surveys administered in 1969, 1976, and 1984, Boyer also reported changes in student responses to a list of "essential outcomes of college." The results were used to emphasize that students have shown increasing individualism in stating their desired college outcomes. Such individualism, in Boyer's view, should be balanced by colleges who bear responsibility for placing greater emphasis on the sense of community or common good.

Finally, in providing a guide to a good college, Boyer included the need for colleges to present themselves honestly to students, to smooth the transition from high school, to state clearly goals and missions, and to "serve individual students while also giving significant attention to community concerns" (p. 288). The list still made no direct mention of student goals. Thus, although the Carnegie report begins with a presentation of student goals, it moves full cycle to base its recommendations on goals and objectives established solely, or primarily, by colleges. However, Boyer implied there was need for a connection between college goals and student goals in reporting, "We found a longing among undergraduates for a more coherent view of knowledge" (p. 85).

As reflected in those recent reports, the tendency to ignore student goals is found throughout the higher education literature. Most research regarding institutional effectiveness takes as its measure of success student acquisition of the institution's values and objectives. Thus, many studies consider *institutional intentions* (e.g., educational mission) and *student outcomes* (e.g., retention rates or grade point averages) without attention to educational processes where these intentions and outcomes interact. Without espousing any particular set of goals as right or wrong, we submit that current research shows that the coherence Boyer claims students long for can be achieved, in part, through consideration of the interaction of student and institutional goals in classroom settings. It seems likely that coherence for students will depend in part on the links between their own goals and those of their colleges.

Additionally, in an era of assessing the success of both students and colleges, student goals may represent an important missing link in assessment efforts. Some colleges that view assessment as a means of improving teaching are in the forefront of using student goals in their work. Alverno College, for example, incorporates the goals of both faculty and students in their curriculum development. Faculty goals were examined and discussed as Alverno reassessed its curriculum, and the emphasis on values that resulted from this process encourages students to develop and examine their own values by thinking about their goals (Earley, Mentkowski, and Schafer 1980). Kean College in Union, New Jersey, requires each major program to develop assessment protocol and procedures. While the assessment approach taken by each program in the college varies widely, each program is expected to incorporate input from both current students and alumni.*

In subsequent chapters, we critique current practice and research concerned with measuring student goals, draw upon recent research in psychology and education to examine potentially related ideas that typically have not been used in research on goals, and suggest a variety of frameworks that might support measurement of the goals students bring to their specific courses. Finally, we suggest how educators might use our newly conceived goal inventory, based on an encompassing framework, to improve teaching and assessment at the course level. In drawing upon a synthesis of related literature to set forth a plan for a goals inventory, we recognize that classroom instructors will have neither the time nor the expertise to construct such an instrument themselves. We provide the rationale and implications as background to the development of an adaptable inventory, tentatively titled the Student Goals Exploration, which we currently are testing in the field, and which should be available in 1990.

*D. Lumsden, Kean College, Union, N.J. 1989, personal communication.

CURRENT TRENDS IN MEASURING COLLEGE STUDENTS' GOALS

Most of the literature dealing with college students' goals is made up of explorations of students' intentions at the time they enter college (Astin, Green, and Korn 1987). Many colleges administer goal surveys to entering students along with other assessments and placement tests. In doing so, they hope to discover the general reasons why students attend college, what they expect to get from attending, and the reasons why they choose a particular institution.

Goal Surveys
and Student Typologies

The most common use of the information in such surveys is for administrative planning. For example, when changes in goals are found among successive cohorts of entering students, some colleges may view this as indicating a need to revise old programs or initiate new ones. In other cases, colleges may expand recruiting efforts to enroll students with goals more in line with college missions.

Another common administrative use of entry-level goal surveys is for *post hoc* studies after college of student satisfaction or self-perceived change. The entry-level items, or slight variants, are provided to upper-class students or recent graduates to estimate the extent to which the college has helped them achieve their goals. Despite this institutional concern, we have found little evidence, either published or in our inquiries of institutional researchers, that colleges use the information they gain from administering pre-entry surveys to improve or individualize classroom instruction.

Researchers probably have paid more attention to student goals than have college administrators and faculty. Like college administrators, however, researchers tend to consider students' entry-level responses to goal statements as relatively fixed. Goal statements such as "to gain exposure to new ideas," "to develop lasting friendships," "to get a better job," or "to prepare for graduate school" are seen as relatively stable orientations. Thus, when researchers include goals in their studies, they often are considered outside of the sphere of influence of the college or academic program the student enters. Because of this perception, researchers frequently classify students according to their major entry-level goals to describe entering students' goal variations by type of program, or to compare groups of students on other measures such as retention rates. Sometimes researchers examine possible

Researchers probably have paid more attention to student goals than have college administrators and faculty.

implications of the fit between institutional goals and student goals.

Components of Existing Instruments

Instruments used to assess student goals frequently are based on general categories of human development such as personal, social, psychological, intellectual, or vocational development. The most common sets of goal statements present up to 10 broad statements intended to tap each type of goal. This brevity and generality is needed in lengthy, multipurpose surveys of entering students. Some common examples of surveys are reprinted in the appendix goal statements used in the Cooperative Institutional Research Program survey (Astin, Green, and Korn 1987), by Educational Testing Service in a recent study (Willingham 1985, pp. 135–36), and in the Student Outcomes Information Services instruments to assess college outcomes (National Center for Higher Education Management Systems 1983).

Learning from earlier experience

Researchers derived many items frequently found in current goal surveys from research with students during earlier decades, using interviews with students of varying aptitudes or from their survey responses. For example, Astin and Nichols (1964), in a study later replicated by Richards (1966), identified the life goals of traditional-age college students. These goals included: prestige, personal happiness, humanistic-cultural, religious, scientific, artistic, hedonistic, altruistic, and athletic success. Analyses of career plans of students scoring differently on such goals revealed significant differences in the life goals of students pursing different careers. One explanation was that a person's choice of vocation is an attempt to find an occupation that will provide the maximum chance of achieving life goals. This idea resulted in links being made among personality theory, goal development, and career choice.

Educators have published other survey items on goals obtained from practical experience with students, but time constraints and the need for generality when collecting entry-level information from diverse student groups seem to doom them to rapid obscurity.

Organizing surveys on goals

Using the goal classifications that predominate in the literature, we have organized the discussion of existing surveys according to personal, social, vocational, and intellectual goals. Because of the growing attention being paid to student deficits in basic skills, however, we note that the intention to improve such skills may constitute a special sub-category of intellectual goals that is included infrequently in lists from 20 years ago. In noting this, we should mention also that there is ambiguity among educators concerning whether some goals, such as "to improve my writing skills," are college-level intellectual goals or personal remedial goals. The confusion is illustrated by the fact that major testing services gather data on such items about basic learning needs prior to college admission, while including others in inventories of college goals.

In table 1 (see next page), we have indicated whether each of various recent studies has included particular goal types.

What's missing from goal surveys?

Researchers have made relatively few attempts to derive goal items anew from student contacts recently. It is possible, however, that freshly written and tested items might capture the goals of today's students better than time-tested categories. It bears noting, too, that in the current "pretest and posttest assessment" data collection used by many colleges there is minimal provision for measuring goal changes over time. Typically, the postcollege surveys for recent graduates or alumni reproduce the list of goals originally presented at college entry. Graduates are not asked, however, for an assessment of currently important goals. Rather, they are instructed to answer retrospectively, according to how important the goal was when they began college (see, for instance, SOIS Recent Alumni Questionnaire).

In addition, although there often is a small space for "other" goals to be added, there seems little encouragement for respondents to add goals not represented in their thinking as entering freshmen. Yet, as freshmen, students may not have clear long-range perspectives and may place more emphasis on personal and social goals than do seniors (Feldman and Newcomb 1969, chap. 4).

Thus alumni surveys leave little room for observing growth. This limitation may be important particularly for mature students who are being asked both as freshmen and as alumni to respond to goal statements originally derived from comments by 17-year-olds. An interesting exception to these

TABLE 1

TYPES OF GOALS INCLUDED IN COMMON GOAL SURVEYS

Researcher or Originator of Study/Date	Target Audience of Survey or Purpose of Study	Personal	Social	Academic	Career
Broad Scale Studies or Surveys					
Astin and Nichols/(1964)	Merit Scholars	X		X	X
Astin et al. (CIRP)/(1966 to 1987)	Entering Freshman	X	X	X	X
Bowen/(1977)	Synthesis/compendium of all college goals	X			
NCHEMS/College Board/(1983)	Outcome studies	X	X	X	X
Pace/(1975)	College students	X	X	X	X
Willingham/(1985)	Liberal arts colleges	X	X	X	X
Studies in Specific Contexts					
Augustin/(1985)	Adult students	X			
Cohen, A./(1986)	Community college students	X			X
Doan and Verroye/(1985)	Community college students	X		X	X
Elfner et al./(1985)	College students			X	X
Friedlander/(1982)	Community college students			X	
Friedlander/(1986)	Community college students			X	X
Friedlander and Grocke/(1985)	Community college students			X	X
Gill and Fruehling/(1979)	College students	X	X	X	X
Katchadourian and Boli/(1985)	Stanford U. students			X	X
Los Angeles Harbor College/(1982)	Community college students	X	X		X
Moss/(1985)	Community college students			X	
Otto/(1980)	Community college students	X	X		X
Romano/(1985)	Community college students	X	X	X	X
Scott, T./(1980)	College-bound students	X		X	X
Shearon/(1980)	Community and technical college students	X	X		
Weissberg et al./(1982)	College students	X	X	X	

generalizations is an alumni survey instrument currently used by a number of colleges that asks about abilities important after college completion*.

Personal Goals

Since almost any aspect of personal development may continue, or begin, during college, the list of potential student goals in the personal domain is lengthy. Also, statements of personal goals may be very broad, or very specific. On the one hand, students frequently are asked to respond to broad compound statements such as "to learn about myself, my values, and my life's goals." On the other hand, a more specific statement may be a survey item such as, "to increase my self-confidence in the workplace."

Institutional researchers conducting surveys for administrative purposes usually select from the personal domain those goals that they believe are most important to the particular type of student, or to the college mission that characterizes their institution. To illustrate, it is unlikely that a goal such as "to get away from home," or "to gain independence from my parents," would apply if most students surveyed were adult students attending a local community college. For such students, a personal goal such as "to learn to manage my time effectively" might have quite a different meaning than it does for traditional-age college students.

Because of student diversity, observers do not always agree on which goals to classify as personal. Note, for example, that although students are asked to say what is important to them personally, many items in the CIRP questionnaire (see appendix a-1) could be classified as academic, vocational, or social goals.

In contrast to educational practitioners, researchers are likely to classify as personal goal statements those items that are related to theoretical foundations of their investigation or problem. Since many student goal statements now in use originated with researchers involved in psychologically based studies (e.g., Astin and Panos 1969; Holland 1966), it is not surprising that some goal inventories are heavily laden with personal goal items.

---

*J. Pettit, Georgetown University, Washington, D.C. 1989, personal communication.

Social Goals

Social development among college students seldom has proceeded in the direction predicted, or even desired, by parents or educators. Early studies of college students documented their increasing liberalism, decreasing religiousness, and increasing hedonism that brought disapproval from elders (Feldman and Newcomb 1969). Yet, many outcomes typically classed as hedonistic probably never were conscious goals for students. Students surveyed as experiencing such outcomes more likely originally endorsed goals such as "to become more at ease in a social group."

Acceptable social development changes over time with shifting social norms. Some documented college outcomes that once violated societal standards are accepted today as gains in social maturity. Astin and Nichols (1964) classified as "hedonistic" a group of student goals that included being well-off financially, having the time and means to enjoy life, and avoiding hard work. While these are goals fitting the general definition of hedonism since they are likely to bring pleasure, in the stress-conscious 1980s they might be considered socially acceptable goals.

Social goals may not be clearly separated from personal goals. And because social interaction increasingly centers on the workplace, social goals may not be distinct from vocational goals. As with personal goals, choices of the many social items one might include on a survey of goals often are specific to a situation. For example, researchers have not included consistently both personal and social goals when studying student goals in commuter colleges, particularly community colleges. It is assumed that adult students may achieve their social goals at home or at work, focusing only on academic goals when they come to campus.

In general, college graduates of all ages seem to have learned the social and cultural sophistication they need for adult life and work, even though they could not articulate these goals as entering students.

Vocational Goals

Over the years, a great deal of research centered upon students' career or vocational goals and the related issue of choosing a major field of study (Tiedeman and O'Hara 1963; Gordon 1984). Nearly all goal surveys ask students to report vocational or career goals on at least three levels. Typically, for example, students are asked the *highest degree* they expect to pursue, the *subject or major field* they are likely to choose, and the *career* they plan to pursue. These reports have attracted increasing attention as contemporary students not only place more emphasis on career goals than did their counterparts 20 years ago, but also cite economic (rather than altruistic or prestige) reasons for career choices (Astin, Green, and Korn 1987).

Although the public attaches high credibility to reports of vocational goals of entering students, it is likely that the vocational goals and educational aspirations expressed in response to these questions are the least stable of all goal areas. There are two reasons for this:

1. Beyond the undergraduate degrees, most new students probably do not understand the American educational credentialling system well enough to make meaningful responses to the string of degree abbreviations with which they are presented in a typical goal survey.
2. A substantial literature on choice of major and career during the undergraduate years indicates that students frequently change their plans after they enter college (Astin and Panos 1969; Davis 1965; Fenske and Scott 1973; Holland and Whitney 1968).

For example, based on a national sample of about 13,000 students at two- and four-year institutions more than a decade ago, Fenske and Scott found that the majority of students indeed do make changes. The figure at two-year institutions for those students retaining their original degree aspirations was 42.8 percent for males and 47.8 percent for females. In the four-year institutions, only 39.7 percent of survey respondents maintained the same field of study, or vocation.

In another study, based on data gathered from a large national sample between 1961 and 1965, researchers also found that choices of major or career were very unstable over four college years, with only 25 percent choosing the same career in 1965 as they had in 1961 (Astin and Panos 1969). In a more recent summary, Gordon (1984, p. 46) reports that although about 75 percent of students ostensibly have decided on a major or career in their first year of college, most change their plans during the college years.

Student career goal survey limits
The career goals stated by students entering college probably are limited by the lists of traditional careers devised by edu-

cational researchers. In many surveys, 10 familiar career fields—business, college teaching, engineering, homemaking, law, medicine, nursing, school teaching, scientific research, and social work—account for nearly 60 percent of freshmen career choices. Many emerging, or less well-known occupations (which students may be unaware of), are unlikely to be chosen.

An unfortunate ancillary to the assumption that career choices are stable is that the public recently has tended to make personnel decisions and judgments about the characteristics of people who enter certain occupations (such as public school teaching), on the basis of their career intention at the time of college admission or entrance.

Limits to survey questions

Many student development experts probably would agree that asking entering traditional-age students about vocational goals is naive. For example, Chickering (1969) pointed out that 18-year-olds are far more concerned with their social and physical development than about future careers. Perry (1970) found that college freshmen often thought in dual terms, determining what is good and bad, right and wrong, attractive and unattractive, based on their parents' or teachers' views. Thus, students were unable to make an independent synthesis of vocational information as well at college entrance as they were after they had learned to entertain a wide variety of views.

Some of the movement between academic majors is related undoubtedly to students' reassessment of their abilities. For example, a researcher ties some of the movements between major fields to academic grades. In his study at several colleges, students with low freshman grades were more likely to change majors to a department viewed as more lenient in grading, while students with high grades who changed sometimes moved to departments with stricter grading standards (Willingham 1985, p. 129).

At the same time, influences on students may change during college. Parents, work experience, and job trends are the most important influences on career choices in the freshman year. But, in later years, fellow students, course work, and other influences become more prominent (Willingham 1985, p. 78).

Academic Goals and Intellectual Goals

Although many authors use the terms "academic goals" and "intellectual goals" interchangeably, we distinguish here between these two types of goals on the basis of the motivations that frequently accompany them. "Intellectual goals" usually are perceived by educators to stem from human curiosity or intrinsic motivation to learn. In contrast, "academic goals" may be viewed as more functional and situational.

The rewards garnered when academic goals are achieved successfully are associated more directly with receiving a degree and its associated status and privileges including employment or admission to the next educational level. Students who endorse statements such as "I want to learn to think logically," "I want to immerse myself in the world of ideas," or "I want to learn more about how humans have governed themselves in this world," have endorsed an intellectual goal even though some of their observable behavior may seem utilitarian. Students who endorse a statement like "It is important for me to graduate from college," have endorsed only an academic goal, and it is more difficult to know whether this goal has intrinsic intellectual components.

Another distinction between intellectual and academic goals is based on origin. Students who endorse academic goals may have accepted those goals from parents or society and are willing to pursue them. In contrast, intellectual goals are more likely to originate within oneself. The intellectual goal may be acquired through a socialization process but, unlike the academic goal, it probably will not disappear with a change in context. In short, academic goals often are short-term and specific to a situation, while intellectual goals are seen more as socialized characteristics learned over a long period of time.

The distinction made here between intellectual and academic goals is stressed because such distinctions often do not appear in the surveys themselves. While goal items on surveys focusing on personal, social, and vocational goals are numerous and often quite specific, those items designed to explore academic and/or intellectual goals appear infrequently, and most often are very general. Of the two, academic goal questions are more frequent. When goal items designated "intellectual" appear at all, they are stated in such broad terms ("to develop a meaningful philosophy of life") that their ability to separate groups of students in any useful way is questionable.

Studies show that college attendance goals which are included in surveys are very important to many students and, hence, discriminate minimally among those who attend college. In fact, the group mean scores among new freshmen for most such items range from 3.7 to 4.0 on a four-point scale. In contrast, there is a good deal more variance on personal, social, and vocational goals.

Whatever the reasons for the underdevelopment of survey items tapping specific academic and intellectual goals, it remains that in their present forms, the broad, nonspecific academic and intellectual goals measures included in current goals instruments are of limited use to researchers, administrators, and teachers alike. Higher education is an intellectual enterprise. Hence, the vagueness of current goals instruments is puzzling. Time constraints in surveying students provides a partial explanation, at best.

Can students articulate specific goals?

Perhaps educational researchers have conceptualized academic and intellectual goals broadly because they have little faith in the student's ability to articulate more specific goals. Though inconclusive, evidence suggests that students can articulate both academic and intellectual goals. In exploratory research, we asked 109 students in introductory courses two questions:

What do you think your instructor most wants you to learn in this course?

Are those same goals the ones that you want to learn?

Students identified those specific course goals from a list that were most important to them and to their instructors. This small, though probably typical, group of students from eight different colleges selected goals for courses that correlated reasonably well (.28 to .60) with those they espoused for college. In addition, many students were able to discuss their course level goals with the interviewer and identify the extent to which they felt their goals diverged from those of their teachers (Stark, Lowther et al. 1988).

On the other hand, it was clear that the students still were developing the ability to articulate their intellectual goals. We were struck with the stages others have described for vocational development including: 1) exploration, 2) crystallization, 3) choice, 4) clarification (Tiedeman and O'Hara 1963). We wondered why those concerned with intellectual development had not attempted to test the existence of similar stages in the development of intellectual goals.

Fuzzy Boundaries

The boundaries between the types of college goals are fuzzy. It is debatable, for example, whether the goal of "increasing my enjoyment of literature" is an intellectual goal or a personal goal. The preferred classification may depend upon the characteristics of student background and college context. A goal such as "to discuss ideas with other learners" could stem from either social or intellectual motivations. In the same way, a number of goals in the citizenship development area could be seen as equally intellectual, or social.

Fuzziness also occurs in goal statements identifying a desired skill that perhaps is useful on various intellectual levels. Commitment to the goal of improving skills in areas such as reading or writing, for example, signifies a different level of academic development than, say, learning to analyze literary works. However, achievement of the latter presumes mastery of the former.

Finally, only a fine line distinguishes career exploration from personal development. Even for students with a firm vocational choice, the goals of financial security, prestige as an authority in a field, and altruism are blended in different proportions, depending on the nature of the career. Classification of students into groups on the basis of such indistinct categories has been problematic throughout the development and use of goals surveys. The discussion of student typologies that follows takes a critical look at the strengths and weaknesses of attempts to categorize students.

One root of the difficulty in accurately and consistently identifying students perhaps is the fact that many can be assigned to different categories at different times.

Typologies

Indistinct categories notwithstanding, educators have developed numerous typologies of students based on their goals, or related attitudes and behaviors. Usually, researchers approached the issue of student goals by developing strategies to classify students into various types through survey responses. Typologies assume that students who respond in like fashion to questionnaires either possess similar goals, exhibit similar behavior, or both. Further, it is assumed that groups of students with similar goals will exhibit similar reactions to the general college experience, and that these reactions will differ substantially from those with other goals.

A number of student typologies have been useful in categorizing the diverse array of students attending colleges and universities. Research on student typologies has been used to predict academic major, college choice, and vocational choice. For example, studies of goal and typologies often are used for student counseling purposes.

Increased access to computer programs that perform complex analyses by grouping individual survey responses into similar patterns may increase the number and accuracy of typologies based on goals or data from other types of surveys. Stage (1988) discusses this improved capability and its potential for linking goals, typologies, and outcomes.

Most commonly, typologies are based on goal types, or other broad categories such as intellectual or vocational orientations. Typologies exhibit clear differences, however, when they stem from researchers' own predilections. For example, Clark and Trow's (1966) well-known typology was based on the notion of student sub-cultures, yet only a few studies have attempted to validate the existence of such sub-cultures. This classification was adapted by the Educational Testing Service into four statements for use in the College Student Questionnaires (1971). As might be expected, responses to these statements reflected students' personal philosophies of higher education rather than their social groupings into sub-cultures. Thus, the classification served as four broad quasi-goal statements.

Typology heyday

The heyday of typology building was probably in the mid-1960s, when an increasingly heterogeneous student body, coupled with the relatively experimental atmosphere of the decade, rendered the environment receptive to such explorations. Starting from different theoretical frameworks, several prominent typologies focused on various personality traits of students. Feldman and Newcomb (1969), Keniston (1966), and Holland (1966) created typologies based on personality types, while Hackman and Taber (1979) described several types of successful and unsuccessful students.

Another group of typologies was aimed at establishing links between personality types and educational and vocational goals. Researchers conducted a study of educational and vocational plans using a freshman questionnaire (N = 4,815), repeatedly measuring 1,475 seniors at eight diverse institutions. The authors reported that while students of nine different types were attracted to different types of majors, each student shared some attributes of several types (Wilson, Gaff,

Dienst, Wood, and Bavry 1975, pp. 112, 117). The nine characteristics were:

intellectual	hip nonconformist
academic	athletic
activist	social
vocational	political
artistic	

Similarly, Heist and Yonge prepared the Omnibus Personality Inventory for use with college students and identified eight distinct intellectual dispositions. (Wilson, Gaff, Dienst, Wood, and Bavry 1975, p. 135).

The categories are of interest because the typology is one of the few that has focused on intellectual growth. They included:

1. broad intrinsic interests with strong literary an aesthetic perspectives
2. intrinsic interests oriented toward dealing with concepts and abstractions
3. intellectuality emphasizing problem-solving and rational thinking
4. intellectuality tempered by orientation to achievement and a disciplinary focus
5. interest in academic matters and achievement, but as a means toward an end
6. learning orientation with vocational and practical emphases
7. nonintellectual, with no interest in ideas, or literary, and aesthetic matters
8. anti-intellectual, but not uninterested in tangibles and learning the practical (Wilson et al. 1975, pp. 135-36).

Typologies designed explicitly for cross-institutional comparisons also have been developed. The Educational Testing Service's College Student Questionnaire utilized seven different scales to categorize freshmen according to their backgrounds and interests. These included:

family independence	cultural sophistication
peer independence	motivation for grades
liberalism	family social status
social conscience	

A primary use of the scales was to compare an institution's freshman class profile with those generated at similar colleges (ETS 1971).

As the student population has expanded to include large numbers of part-time adult and/or commuter students, some researchers have responded by creating new typologies to represent this group more accurately. The work of Sheldon and Grafton (1982), for example, focused on characterizing community college students according to their practical reasons for attending college. Yet, considering the fact that over half of higher education's undergraduates now attend community colleges, it is clear that not nearly enough work has been done to identify accurately the goals of community college students.

The most recent typologies have broken little new ground but serve, instead, to update earlier ones. For example, the intellectual and career orientations which define Katchadourian and Boli's (1985) categorization of Stanford University undergraduates serve to reinforce the old Clark-Trow classification. While researchers of student characteristics generally stressed the permeability of classification boundaries, Katchadourian and Boli's work reemphasized the fact that most students are not described completely by any one profile presented in typologies of this type. In the admittedly restricted population of Stanford undergraduates, most students exhibit some characteristics of each type: strivers, careerists, intellectuals, and unconnecteds.

The trouble with classifying . . .

One root of the difficulty in accurately and consistently identifying students perhaps is the fact that many can be assigned to different categories at different times. Such a tendency seems particularly prevalent in the college years. "Students tend to become more variable in their self-concepts during the four years following matriculation" (Astin 1978, p. 34). Yet, because educational researchers seldom are explicit about students' proclivity for change, typologies often are criticized as incorrectly and unfairly "pigeon-holing," or stereotyping students.

Another part of the difficulty is that the number of dimensions on which a classification is based is limited. It may fail

TABLE 2
TYPOLOGIES IN COMPARISON

	Careerist	Intellectual	Striver	Unconnected	Other
Clark and Trow (1966)	Vocational subculture	Academic subculture	—	—	Collegiate subculture (Noncon-formist subculture)
Warren (1966, 1968)	Vocational, Uncommitted orientations	Academic, Intel-lectual orientations		(Undirected orientation)	Autonomous, Social protest, Tra-ditional, Self-centered, Conformist orientations
Pemberton (1963)	Technical-vocational orientation	Academic-theoretical orientation	—	—	Academic conformity, Noncon-formity, Social-service orientations
Keniston (1966)	Apprentice	Professionalist	—	(Disaffiliate)	Activist, Big man on campus, Underachiever, Gentleman-in-waiting
Newcomb, Koenig, Flacks, and Warwick (1967)		Scholar	(Leader)		Creative individualist, Wild one, Political activist, Social group
Holland (1966, 1973)	(Enterprising personality)	Investigative personality	—	—	Realistic, Social, Conventional, Artistic personalities
Korn (1968)	Career group	Intellectual interests group	—	—	Grades group
Allport-Vernon-Lindzey (1960)	Economic type	Theoretical, Aesthetic types	—	—	Social, Political, Religious types

Note: Parentheses indicate partial correspondence of categories.
Source: Katchadourian and Boli 1985.

to encompass in a meaningful way the wide variety of students' goals that actually exist.

Katchadourian and Boli provide a summary of typologies
in comparison with their own (1985, p. 41), which we have
reproduced here as table 2. (In appendix 3, we provide more
detail regarding the descriptions of their typologies and
others.)

Goals and Outcomes

Goals and outcomes are related intricately. In fact, goal statements, traditionally thought of as measuring characteristics
of entering students, also can be translated into outcomes
representing facets of social, personal, academic, or intellectual development. The reverse translation also can be made.
(In short, we can conceive of goals as either independent variables or dependent variables.) As a result, various lists of
desired college outcomes may be converted into lists of goals.

Such a conversion is seen readily in the construction of the SOIS Questionnaires (NCHEMS/College Board) from an already-established list of outcomes (Lenning et al. 1977, p. 27). It is easy to imagine the translation of a goal statement such as "to improve my social and economic status" to an outcome statement that is measured in concrete terms after graduation.

More specific lists of outcomes also may lend themselves to conversion into goal statements; yet, to date, such translations are not made. One reason may be difficulties in measuring the outcomes. For example, some parts of the Astin, Panos, and Creager classification (1967), which focus on cognitive and affective outcomes, have yet to be tapped for this purpose. It remains problematic to measure affective outcomes such as "enjoyment of literature," or "improvement of self-image." Although these outcomes are quite legitimate college goals, nevertheless, researchers continue to use broader typologies as guides when focusing intensively on academic goals.

For example, in measuring outcomes, the National Center for Research to Improve Postsecondary Teaching and Learning placed the focus on the academic setting (Alexander and Stark 1986, table 3), but behavioral measures were added to the Astin et al. classification. In addition to measurement difficulties, researchers' reluctance to convert systematically measurement of outcomes into goal statements well may stem from uncertainty about whether students could interpret satisfactorily such goals. Studies at Alverno College indicate that, at least in one setting, students can, and do, participate in goal-setting and self-assessment of their progress (Mentkowski and Loacker 1985). Clearly, the ability of students to do so needs to be further tested in a variety of colleges.

Typologies and Vocational Goals
Typologies are extremely popular in attempts to understand and predict student vocational choice. The way students initially select a field of study or a vocation involves a complicated process incorporating a number of variables including ability, personality type and interests, self-perception, parental influence, peer influence, socioeconomic status, work experience, job trends, educational opportunity, and a vision of desired life style (Bomotti 1987, p. 18).

TABLE 3
NCRIPTAL'S OUTCOME FRAMEWORK

Form of Measurement	Academic Outcome
Cognitive	Achievment (facts, principles, ideas, skills)
	Critical-thinking skills
	Problem-solving skills
Motivational	Satisfaction with college
	Involvement/effort
	Motivation
	Self-efficacy
Behavioral	Career and life goal exploration
	Exploration of diversity
	Persistence
	Relationships with faculty

Source: Alexander and Stark 1986.

Despite that complexity, however, theories that attempt to explain or illuminate the phenomenon of vocational choice frequently are variations on the theme of "person-environment fit" or personality theory. Although not all were developed specifically for use in educational settings, several vocational theories have evolved into typologies sometimes used by educators and researchers as related to student goals, or even as proxies for them.

Several theories emphasizing the "person" side of the person-environment fit equation hold that people seek jobs (or, presumably, majors while in college) that are consistent with their personal traits (Brown, Brooks et al. 1984). Such a view is associated closely with Holland's "Theory of Vocational Personalities and Work Environments." According to this theory, six personality types result from

a characteristic interaction among a variety of cultural and personal forces including peers, biological heredity, parents, social class, culture and the physical environment. Out of this experience, a person learns first to prefer some activities as opposed to others. Later, these activities become strong interests; such interests lead to a special group of competencies. . . . In short, each type has a characteristic repertoire

*of attitudes and skills for coping with environmental prob-
lems and tasks. Different types select and process information in different ways, but all types seek fulfillment by exer-
cising characteristic activities, skills, and talents, and by
striving to achieve special goals"* (Holland 1985, pp. 2-3).

Hence, the choices which students and/or workers make are
seen simply as the product of their environments and the possibilities present in their lives.

Even when vocational aspects do not predominate in a
given goals survey, an element of the vocational often seems
to characterize description of the results. An example is the
Student Orientations Survey (Morstain 1973), which contains
10 scales, two of which focus on the following dimensions:
educational purposes, educational processes, power relationships in classrooms, student peer relations, and public posi-
tion. When the 10 scales are analyzed further, students can
be categorized as having either an *exploratory orientation*
toward their education, seeking to explore ideas of all types
for their intrinsic interest, or a *preparatory orientation*, pursuing education because it is instrumental in achieving career
goals. As in other typologies, the two are not polar opposites.

It is not surprising that students seem to gravitate primarily
toward one or the other orientation since, even in liberal arts
colleges, faculty tend to lean toward one of these categories
as well (Stark and Morstain 1978). Moreover, students who
remain in college longer increasingly resemble their profes-
sors in terms of learning orientation. This tendency clearly
illustrates the propensity of student goals to shift under influence of the college experience (Stark 1975).

Why students shift
While the shifting of student goals is attributed most often
to psychological variables such as increases in motivation or
self-concept, some studies address the sociological issues sur-
rounding this phenomenon. For example, a researcher
recently attempted to show that the environment in collegiate
settings actually reinforces already existing personality types
as measured by Holland's theory (Smart 1985). This research
links a psychological conceptualization of goals to one with
a sociological basis by recognizing the influence of new environments on goals that had been viewed as somewhat stable.
Unlike the somewhat better-established psychological

research on goals, the sociological perspective stresses the cultural and social sides of career choice (Brown et al. 1984). Social class boundaries either may facilitate or truncate choice. In any case, they act as a critical filter to the kind of information, encouragement, and opportunities available to the individual.

For example, when interviewing college students about college and course goals, we found that African-American students and students whose parents had not attended college were more likely than students from more advantaged backgrounds to adopt vocational and practical goals and less likely to choose intellectual and personal college goals (Stark et al. 1988). Some sociological theorists believe that people are steered by socioeconomic factors toward occupational roles that match their social status. Insofar as college students have opportunities to experience new environments, philosophies and cultures, college may serve to minimize the boundaries imposed by these external cultural aspects.

While in many cases personality types or vocational choices have been used to create typologies, the reverse process—using typologies to predict vocational choices—also has occurred. Likewise, student typologies are used to predict student proclivities for one field of study or another. For example, Katchadourian and Boli (1985) found that of their four groups of Stanford students, *careerists* are more likely to plan careers in business, medicine, or engineering. *Intellectuals* gather in the humanities and are less likely to be found in the natural sciences, engineering, medicine, law, or economics. *Strivers* are fairly evenly distributed across the fields, and the *unconnecteds* are highly variable; humanities and law are popular, but so are natural science and engineering. *Unconnecteds* are least likely to choose careers in business, and they are more likely to be undecided, or to make more changes in choice of major than other students.

Summary
Many studies report student goals by college type, or compare the fit between institutional goals and student goals, drawing implications for student choice, attrition, or recruitment. Typologies of students, often based on goals, sometimes are used to predict academic major, college type, and vocational choice. The rationale for such uses is either *psychological* (based in personality theory or developmental theory), or

sociological (based on the influence of the home and college context).

Although frequent change is demonstrated, most studies appear to view as enduring the goals that students bring to college. Longitudinal studies of goals measured over time seldom are conducted to determine the correlates of goal shifts. And, only a few studies relate academic course experiences to goal attainment or to goal change.

The growing diversity of the student population over the last 20 years has created new reasons to examine student goals. The burgeoning community college sector, in particular, with its predominance of part-time and commuter students, calls into question the validity of the person-environment fit models (see Pascarella and Chapman 1983). The result is the birth of a new set of special types and goal instruments, created to characterize more accurately the goals of the community college student (Sheldon and Grafton 1982; Friedlander 1986).

Clearly, classifying orientations toward college is a topic of considerable interest to researchers and of some interest to educational administrators, albeit for different reasons. Yet, the ways in which information about goals is used by colleges and universities to change educational practice is less clear.

Sometimes, measures of goals as entering characteristics become confused with measures of college outcomes. Such may be the case with the public concern arising from data suggesting that entering students' vocational goals are becoming more prominent than their altruistic and philosophic goals. It is easy for the public to confuse information gathered from entering freshmen with the outcomes society desires of college students at graduation. Comparative information actually documenting outcomes or relating them to goals seldom is available, but can become an important aspect of college assessment plans.

In the succeeding chapters we address other broad dilemmas associated with student goals research, including those which follow.

1. The interchange of terms such as goals, needs, values, objectives, and motivations leads to semantic and conceptual confusion.
2. No consistent classification of goal types has been empirically, or logically established. Within the generally recognized types, such as personal, social, and vocational

goals, confusion among levels of goals, such as the continued development of precollegiate basic skills, collegiate-level academic goals, and higher-order intellectual goals, add to the difficulties.

3. Goal studies only rarely include goal attributes such as specificity, clarity, source, commitment, or temporality, that might help to better define goals or relate college experiences to goal attainment.

4. The links between concepts such as goals, motivation, efficacy, and expectancy are not well established.

5. Studies of student goals tend to focus at the college-wide level with little attention to concrete goals associated with selection of specific courses, or to the relationships among students' course goals, instructors' course goals, and course achievement.

GOALS AND THEIR NEGLECTED ATTRIBUTES

What Are Goals?

Considerable confusion exists regarding an appropriate definition of goals. What exactly are goals? What operational definitions allow us to conduct meaningful research about them?

Our use of the term "goal" builds on the definition formulated by Locke, Shaw, Saari, and Latham (1981, p. 126), "A goal is what an individual is trying to accomplish: It is the object, or aim, of an action." This view of a goal as something to be achieved by a person is widespread in the literature (Bandura 1986; Dweck and Leggett 1988; Ford 1986; Klinger 1977; Maehr and Braskamp 1986; Markus and Wurf 1987). This definition is useful for educators since, either at the college level or the course level, it can be related to an observed outcome, but distinguished from the needs, motivations, or expected rewards that cause one to desire the goal. The goal also can be distinguished from the effort put toward its achievement.

Although clearly separate from effort or actions, goals play a crucial role in guiding the activities of individuals as they strive for achievement.

Although clearly separate from effort or actions, goals play a crucial role in guiding the activities of individuals as they strive for achievement. Indeed, a substantial body of empirical research links goal-setting to task performance. This research assumes that goals (that is, aims or intentions) are essential for humans to regulate their own behavior. Furthermore, when researchers view goals as intentions, it is possible to examine their effects on behavior in terms of goal attributes such as specificity, difficulty (challenge), clarity, source (origin), commitment (strength), time (temporality), and the like (Bandura 1986, p. 472; Locke et al. 1981). Much of the social science literature refers to these properties as the "dimensions" of goals. We have accepted the suggestion of an anonymous reviewer to use the word "attribute," reserving the term "dimension" in our discussion for quantitative measures of the attributes.[1]

For example, an individual may be committed strongly to a particular goal but nevertheless find it difficult to attain. A goal may be an aim of one's own choosing, or imposed by some authority. It may be general, like "getting an education," or specific, like learning to solve a mathematical equation. By examining such attributes of goals we can look beyond common broad statements and learn more about what reg-

---

[1] Much of the social science literature refers to these properties as the "dimensions" of goals. We have accepted the suggestion of an anonymous reviewer to use the word "attribute," reserving the term "dimension" in our discussion for quantitative measures of the attributes.

TABLE 4
SOME GOAL ATTRIBUTES

1. *Specificity:* the level of directedness of a goal (Locke, Shaw, Saari, and Latham 1981)
2. *Clarity:* level of ambiguity associated with a goal (ibid.)
3. *Difficulty:* the level of effort required to achieve the goal (ibid.; Huber 1985)
4. *Temporality:* the amount and frequency of feedback expected for a given goal (Manderlink and Harackiewicz)
5. *Importance:* the level of the importance assigned to a goal in relation to other goals in a goal hierarchy (Wicker, Lambert, Richardson, and Kahler 1984)
6. *Ownership:* the source of the goal (Garland 1983; Locke, Frederick, Buckner, and Bobko 1984)
7. *Commitment:* the degree to which the goal motivates behavior (Locke, Shaw, Saari, and Latham 1981)
8. *Stability:* the permanence of a goal over a period of time (Robbins and Patton 1985)

ulates student behavior. Although present in the social science literature, these goal attributes often are neglected by educators and educational researchers. Following, then, is an exploration of recent research that can more clearly define the pertinent dimensions of goals.

Goal Specificity
General goals, which are recognized by goal statements, most often relate to the broad life arenas in which the goals operate. For this reason, almost without exception, most instruments on goals and outcomes designed for surveying college students group items according to such general developmental categories as personal, social, intellectual, or vocational goals. The boundaries between these broad categorizations are blurred, as are the areas of human life they represent; the categories cry out for increased specificity and a clearer description of the links between them.

A slightly different categorization of general goal types results when goals are discussed under the heading of motivation, or when more theoretical concepts are used to classify them. For example, Moen and Doyle (1978) classify goals, or "targets of academic motivation," as 1) material motivation (both economic and physical), 2) psychological motivation (self-esteem, mental stimulation, conscientiousness), and 3) social motivation (esteem, social interaction). In this categorization, career goals are seen as more clearly linked with personal goals, with material well-being and comfort underlying both.

The above categorization was developed by directing students to identify broad college goals. However, when educators and students begin to talk about goals or outcomes at the course and program level, broad goals quickly become more specific. The amount and type of specification needed depends upon the context and the intended use of the information. For example, in referring to general reasons for attending college, a student might endorse a goal statement such as "I want to understand how knowledge is developed." At the more specific level of a science course, the related goal might be "I want to understand how scientists explore the nature of living things."

Some goals identified by Astin and Nichols (1964, chap. 2) could be viewed as more specific sub-goals of college attendance since some goals (for example, humanistic-cultural, altruistic, and prestige) are directed at specific types of developmental targets that lie at the border between the personal and social goal types. Other goals, such as artistic, scientific, and athletic success goals, may represent sub-goals that historically have guided human endeavor, areas of knowledge currently offered in collegiate programs, or intersections between personal and intellectual interests.

Despite the obvious conceptual interdependence between student goals and student outcomes, definitions of outcomes often are much more specific than those developed for goals. Yet, like outcomes, goals can be specific to disciplines, occupations, intellectual growth, and personal or social growth. Specificity is needed badly since the broad goal classifications currently in vogue appear to be of minimal value in understanding student learning.

It is difficult, for example, to know what learning activities will help a student achieve a goal as general as "I wanted to learn more about interesting things." It is somewhat easier when the "interesting things" are narrowed down, such as "I wanted to learn about how people have governed themselves through the years."

Since much of student learning is specific to courses, greater specificity of goals lends itself particularly well to analyses of attitude toward, or performance, in a specific course. Carrying the example above a step further, a course goal might be "to learn how people have governed themselves in Western culture so that I may become an informed voter." At the classroom level, the relevant question is the extent to which effort or learning behavior is indicative of the existence of underlying goals, or, conversely, the extent to which goals control the amount of effort directed at learning tasks. Similarly, at the program level, student satisfaction with the major may lead to goal commitment (Aitken 1982), or the reverse may be true, with goal commitment leading to satisfaction.

The perceived use or desirability of a course—its compatibility with the student's goals—determines to a large extent the amount of effort the student will spend on the course work. Some researchers assert the potential relationship more bluntly, "Teaching effectiveness must be considered in relation to specific desired educational goals" (Wilson et al. 1975, p. 18).

Goal Clarity

Another goal attribute, not totally independent of specificity, is goal clarity. Some goals are abstract and vague while others are extremely concrete. Some writers have termed this dimension "goal quality," or have defined clarity in terms of how "adequate" the goal is for a given purpose (Frewin 1977). According to Frewin, learners often come to college with poorly-defined goals and only later develop the ability to discriminate between multiple alternatives.

They have trouble defining goals because they lack focused self-knowledge. While it is useful to recognize that student ability to conceive of clear goals may vary, the term "quality" may unnecessarily denigrate abstract or vague goals that will become clearer over time. If a purpose of education is to help the learner develop the ability to establish effective goals, one might expect early goals to be abstract or vague. Thus, the definition of clarity in terms of ambiguity level (see table 4) is more useful.

To illustrate, an entering student may articulate a goal such as "to improve my study skills." At a later time, this statement takes on clarity (or reduced ambiguity) as the student recognizes and accepts a goal of "relating new ideas to old ones" when studying.

Goal Difficulty or Challenge

In a review of studies on goals, Locke et al. (1981) found that specific and challenging goals lead to higher performance than easy goals. There also is evidence that this relationship depends on the perceived value of the pay-off (Matsui, Okada, and Mizuguchi l981, p. 57; Terborg 1976, p. 619). Adopting goals which are challenging in *specific* arenas but not overwhelming in general may improve academic performance. Although college educators intuitively believe it important to hold high expectations for students and to encourage them to set high expectations for themselves, we do not yet know how to determine the optimal level of goal difficulty. The optimal level may vary for individuals, and it is related to self-concept as well as to prior learning. For one student a difficult goal might be to write an interesting short story; for another, to write a well-structured paragraph.

Goals and Temporality

A variety of terms are used to characterize the time perspective in which goals are held and during which they are achieved. This distinction between goals that are established for the long-range future or the short-range setting is an important dimension of goals. Such time perspectives are not independent of either the type of goal, or its clarity, specification, or challenge. Ordinarily, longer-range goals focus on broader developmental areas such as career and personal growth; they are more abstract, less specific, and less clear. In contrast, short-range goals more often are concerned with interim steps toward long-range growth (Bandura 1986). Short-term goals provide opportunity for frequent, reinforcing feedback.

In discussing goals for college attendance, and particularly when speaking of utilitarian (or extrinsic) goals, educators usually focus on the eventual outcome or long-range goal (job, degree, and intellectual or social stature acquired), leaving the specific activities or strategies needed to reach the goal unspecified. In contrast, when speaking of interest value (or intrinsic) goals, educators more often focus on the immediate enjoyment received from short-range activities achieved on the way to some endpoint which may remain poorly defined. One could ask whether it is possible that "intrinsic interest value" is the short-range counterpart of the long-range "task value/utility" goal.

Student Cases Compared

To illustrate the possibility for college goals, consider the cases of two types of well-prepared college students studying in the liberal arts and sciences: the professionally-oriented student and the undecided student.

The *professionally-oriented undergraduate student* may have strong and effective short-range goals. They may produce enjoyment in their own right, but it is more important to the student that they simultaneously serve as stepping stones to the longer-range professional school or graduate degree goal.

To the *career-undecided student*, the intrinsic enjoyment value of college learning may be equally strong but, since the longer-range goal remains nonspecific, the short-range learning seems more valued for its own sake.

In those cases, two types of goal-directed behavior may occur simultaneously but in varying strength for the two students. One type is progress toward the long-range goal, the other is toward the short-range goal.

Consider, in a totally different context, *underprepared college students* who have not yet established even short-term goals to help regulate learning behavior. Although counseling techniques may help such students to establish and successfully complete short-range goals ("to improve my self-confidence in mathematics") on the route to longer-range goals ("to interpret numerical data correctly"), the long-range goals may remain undefined indefinitely. Although clearly relevant in these very different cases, the relationship of the time orientations seems not to have been incorporated in various classifications of college student goals.

Goal Importance

Long-term, general goals to which individuals are strongly committed usually also incorporate shorter-range, more specific subgoals which serve as instrumental goals, or building blocks. When feedback is given, it is usually in relation to shorter-term goals, since long-term goals usually are not achieved at the time of measurement. The relative ease with which short-term goals are assessed, then, helps students adjust their expectations and self-image to set increasingly clearer and more realistic goals.

However, when short-term goals do not adequately advance students toward their long-term goals, they may not foster achievement of appropriate long-term goals (Fuchs and Fuchs 1985). This may be typified by the behavior of students enrolled in mandatory courses which, in their view, are not linked to their own long-term goals. In such cases, the need for clarification and articulation between the short-term learning tasks assigned and the longer-term goals set by the students themselves becomes quite obvious. In brief, the student needs to create a hierarchy of goals with short-term goals taking on added importance, but with the long-term goals kept clearly in view.

Commonly, the potential outcomes, or rewards, that are assumed to result from achieving goals are classified as extrinsic and intrinsic. Other possible outcomes include the social desirability of the goal (i.e., the social approbation that results from its achievement) or, alternatively, the negative value of avoiding failure to achieve.

In an early version of an instrument designed to measure classroom level motivational orientations, the Motivated Strategies for Learning Questionnaire (MSLQ), Pintrich, McKeachie et al. (1988) constructed a scale that they label "social desirability." It tapped what might equally well be called "work ethic enculturation." The scale items seem to characterize students who have learned to perform in the classroom and who persist in studying hard based on family values.

A statement commonly endorsed by such students is, "Even when study materials are dull or uninteresting, I believe I should keep working until I am finished." The extrinsic motivation here, of course, is either to get positive reinforcement from important others, or to escape negative reinforcement, or punishment. Viewed in this way, extrinsic motivation causes the goal of studying to become most important in a hierarchy of many competing goals. Perhaps such a goal, based on a sense of duty or avoidance, is the shortest range goal of all since it provides neither clear long- range focus, nor short-term personal enjoyment. In brief, neither intrinsic nor extrinsic rewards are received. In any case, the examples that are obvious in the college context highlight the importance of considering the time perspective in which goals are viewed as related to goal importance.

Goal Ownership, Source, or Origin

Goals are established by an individual (voluntary goals) or they are imposed or assigned by other persons (assigned goals). Yet, goals seldom are purely one or the other; instead, they vary along a continuum. While students may establish their career goals independently, they find it difficult to ignore what their family and peer group consider desirable among varied careers and life styles. In fact, among traditional-age college students, goals assigned by parents or peer group are common. Yet the ability to set one's own goals is important (Showers and Cantor 1985), and its achievement is quite possibly an important developmental milestone.

Goal Commitment and Stability

Although affected by other attributes, goal commitment, or strength (sometimes referred to as tenacity), often is related most closely to goal origin (source). Typically, commitment to self-established goals is stronger than commitment to assigned goals. On the other hand, goals assigned by others often are strongly held, particularly in cases where extrinsic rewards are very strong or acceptance is very firm. Long-range goals to which individuals have weak commitment, or which are not of their own choosing (minimal ownership), are likely to be changeable rather than stable.

Locke et al. (1981) make a distinction between the concepts of goal acceptance and commitment that seems particularly important in education. Commitment does not require a specific source; the goal may be devised personally, or externally imposed. Acceptance implies that the goal assigned by another person or agency was accepted as if it was self-generated. This definition speaks to one common concern about college students—namely, that certain academic goals, often assigned by others, may be insufficiently accepted to direct behavior toward that goal when competing goals are present.

The idea of multiple goals of varying strength may provide the underlying basis for the common classification of college student goals into groups classified as social, personal, intellectual, or vocational. Most students possess some of each type, but hold them with varying commitment.

In his study of student success in liberal arts colleges, Willingham (1985) concluded that beyond Scholastic Aptitude Test scores and high school grades, *productivity* was the single most important factor accounting for success in college. He defined productivity, based on faculty reports, student self-reports, and college records, as the characteristic of perseverance at the task of college work. Such perseverance seems characteristic of strong goal commitment.

Perhaps the opposite case is *nondirectedness*, in which a student's educational goals are so weak that they have little or no regulating effect on relevant behavior. This nondirected state often is reported by counselors and teachers as disproportionately common among underprepared or disadvantaged students. This may be related to students' expectations, their self-concept, their possession of adequate learning strategies, or all of these.

Summary

Goals possess multiple attributes, although they are not independent. Existing instruments to assess and describe college student goals have not yet explored, or taken advantage of, the relationship among goal attributes which are very likely related to student academic development.

GOALS AND RELATED IDEAS

Much research leading to student goal instruments used currently was done in the 1960s and 1970s. Personality theory or person-environment fit theories (Stern 1970; Walsh 1973) often formed the bases for such studies. Recently, new findings in cognitive psychology have provided improved understanding of goal-related concepts such as motivation, efficacy, and expectancy (McKeachie et al. 1986). Since these emerging ideas frequently were not linked to student goals, recent higher education literature has failed to keep pace with basic research.

Viewing goals as self-regulators can provide an organizing framework for research involving the academic behavior of college students.

Similarly, knowledge about goals was linked only partially with other rapidly developing areas of research on patterns of college student growth and behavior. For example, research on relating student attrition to academic and social integration (Tinto 1975; 1987), the recently developed ability to measure the quality of student effort (Pace 1984), summaries of learning style research (Claxton and Murrell 1987), and the work of several researchers on the value of informal faculty-student interaction (Pascarella et al. 1980; Wilson et al. 1975), often have proceeded unconcerned with student goals.

To assist others in making these important links, this chapter first will explore potentially fruitful relations between student goals and ideas emerging in other disciplines. Second, it will relate findings and speculations about student goals to the proliferating work of higher education scholars who use eclectic research approaches rather than orthodox methods of psychology or sociology.

Connections in Cognitive Research

Recently, cognitive perspectives influenced research on goal-setting (Bandura 1986; Locke et al. 1981; Markus and Wurf 1987; Showers and Cantor 1985). Cognitive psychologists view goals as part of the self-concept that assists in self-management; in other words, they help individuals control and regulate their actions. Goals act as regulators of human action because they are the objects, or aims, of those actions (Locke et al. 1981, p. 126). "The ultimate point about goals . . . is that they affect behavior" (Maehr 1984, p. 130).

Considering goals important in an individual's self-regulatory process suggests several questions:

- How are goals selected?
- What influences the choice?
- What plans are used to achieve goals?

- What is the role of self-assessment?
- What is the relation of goals to performance?

In reviewing how self-concept guides and controls behavior, Markus and Wurf (1987) address a number of those questions in their discussion of self-regulatory processes from childhood to young adulthood. Based on their discussion, we sense that viewing goals as self-regulators can provide an organizing framework for research involving the academic behavior of college students. Of course, other factors such as culture, social environment, and individual needs also influence collegiate behavior. Yet, during college, a period of intense "reflective self-consciousness" (Bandura 1986), students examine what they think, feel, and believe about themselves. These "possible selves," as Markus and Wurf suggest, are powerful regulators of human behavior. Improved knowledge of students' goals can help us develop a more comprehensive picture of self-regulatory behavior during the college years.

Goals and Self-Regulation

Markus and Wurf suggest that three processes are involved in self-regulation: setting goals, preparing mentally for action, and establishing a cycle of self-monitoring behavior. The following summary is based on their review.

Setting goals.

If goals help individuals to regulate their own action, it is important to understand how people select goals. Three factors contribute to the selection process: 1) expectations, 2) affective factors, motives or values, and 3) desired self-images. Relevant concepts from the work of Bandura (1986) assist in understanding expectations. Bandura implies that a person's behavior is determined both by "outcome expectancies" (certain actions will result in certain outcomes), and by "efficacy expectancies" (whether the person thinks she/he can do what is necessary for the desired outcome). This research suggests that individuals will select goals they can expect to achieve.

Important factors in goal setting (those that psychologists and educators call "affective") include needs, motives, and values. Needs are defined as diffuse, innate motivators of behavior. Motives are learned and more specific than needs. Values (or incentives) are conscious and more specific than either needs or motives. Students' choices of goals may reflect their needs, motives, values, or a combination of these.

A person's self-image also contributes to goal-setting. Following research on life tasks and ideal selves (Cantor et al. 1987), Markus and Wurf suggested that people may select goals that continue self-definitions based on their personal and social histories.

Preparing cognitively for action.

Goals are not achieved through wishful thinking. Rather, a person must plan the actions which, in his or her judgment, will lead to attaining goals. Markus and Wurf point out that these conscious plans depend upon the person's knowledge of useful strategies to achieve goals, and about how to organize strategies. In academic endeavors, useful strategies may be broad and abstract, such as allocating ample study time, or they may be concrete and specific, such as attempting to solve increasingly difficult mathematical problems. While previous academic preparation is necessary for academic achievement, the student also must possess a repertoire of learning strategies relevant to achieving specific goals.

Researchers built on those ideas and perspectives in studies that jointly explored students' motivation and the learning strategies they use in courses (procedural strategies, and strategies such as self-monitoring) (Pintrich et al. 1988).

Cycles of self-monitoring behavior.

In the final phase of the self-regulation process, individuals implement and evaluate actions they have chosen to achieve their goals. Markus and Wurf describe how implementation can initiate a cycle of mental activities that provide self-knowledge. These activities (behaving, monitoring, judging the effectiveness of behavior, and self-evaluating) provide a response to the question, "How am I doing in pursuit of my goals?"

The process of evaluating actions in relation to goals may yield a variety of strong feelings that provide people with a measure of progress toward their goals: joy, satisfaction, anxiety, disappointment, anger, fear, and apprehension (Klinger 1977). As a consequence, students may retain previously selected goals and strategies, or they may choose new goals or actions. The student who makes good progress toward solving word problems in mathematics may persist in the successful study technique. Another student, failing to understand economics, may revise a goal of entering a business field.

Based on those recent theories, it seems fruitful to view college student goals as changeable attributes that assist in self- management. Within this framework, researchers can examine the academic actions of students (deciding to attend college, choosing a college, selecting a major, electing courses, and doing course work) in relation to their goals. It also is possible to study how student goals may change as a result of these experiences.

Goals and Motivations

The value of attaining a goal (expectancy) also influences goal choice. When the goal is valued highly, the commitment to either a self-generated or assigned goal is likely to be stronger. Along with other researchers, McKeachie, Pintrich, Lin, and Smith (1986) assume that student motivations to reach goals fit into two primary motivating components which they call "task value" and "interest value."

Briefly defined, "task value" (sometimes referred to as "extrinsic" goal motivation, or "utility") is concerned with a person's perception of the usefulness of the goal outcome. "Interest value" (sometimes called "intrinsic" goal motiva- tion) is concerned with a person's perceptions of the inherent challenge or enjoyment from attaining the goal, or pursuing related activities. To avoid confusion with other meanings of value, we will use the terms "extrinsic" and "intrinsic" mot- ivation in this discussion.

Investigators of broad college student goals often have divided entering students' goals along lines of intrinsic and extrinsic value similar to those described by McKeachie and colleagues. In fact, one basis for constructing several of the classifications reviewed in chapter 2 is the relative importance of intrinsic and extrinsic motivation. Based on survey ques- tions related to broad college goals, a large group of students are reported to enroll in college because they believe the results will be useful, particularly with regard to a career or financial security (Astin et al. 1986).

A smaller group is referred to as being challenged by the intrinsic motivation of college attendance, sometimes referred to as "learning for learning's sake." The division here parallels the "preparatory" and "exploratory" orientations outlined by Stark and Morstain (1978) for students in liberal arts colleges.

And yet one might question whether the division between utility and enjoyment is real, as Dressel and Marcus (1982) did. They believed that intrinsic motivations to learn for learning's sake really do have task value, or utility. Their utility is the enjoyment the student experiences.

Why do students attend college?

Student goals in attending college have many attributes; they are not one-dimensional. Even the short-term goal of attending college can be viewed as a strategy directed toward achievement of multiple, broad, long-range goals. And, once attending college, the broad goals and motivations students developed earlier may be less important in regulating behavior than the goals they bring to specific courses.

Realistically, as shown in McKeachie's work at the classroom level, aspects of both extrinsic and intrinsic motivators also come into play in student actions at the course level. In a manner parallel to broader goals, goals for particular courses are based on students' knowledge about themselves, general knowledge about the course and instructor, learning skills, self-confidence, and self-monitoring strategies.

Such factors result in expectancies for each course that may differ from those for college success. The explorations of psychologists often are focused on specific tasks within courses. Among the possible causal relationships at this level, student goal orientation and student self-efficacy potentially can interact with anxiety about tests and competence in performing tasks to produce the "task value" and expectancy for success. These, in turn, influence achievement and academic persistence (McKeachie et al. 1986, p. 44).

The major theme of this research is that "motivational and cognitive variables interact in such intimate conjunction that they must be jointly considered in any comprehensive theory of student learning and thinking" (McKeachie, November 1987, p. 3). These researchers refer to this complex interaction as "motivational orientations."

In studying learning tasks, McKeachie's research team includes not only expectancies, but also an assessment of the student's self-efficacy, or perception of his/her own preparedness or ability to achieve the goal. Goal setting is affected by past performance, and a person's expectation of success also is based on that performance. Test anxiety, for example, may result from a realistic appraisal of one's ability to succeed on tests based on previous test results. In this view, self-efficacy helps to predict course performance, as do task value and anxiety. A dimension of expectancy is perceived self-competence; another is control. Learning is promoted by personal control of learning tasks and strategies.

The Motivated Strategies Learning Questionnaire assesses college students' motivational orientations and their use of different self-regulatory learning strategies (Pintrich et al. 1988). The questionnaire's section on *motivation* consists of items assessing the value students believe a course has for them, their beliefs about their ability to succeed, and their anxiety about tests. The *learning strategy* section includes items addressing students' use of varied cognitive and organizing strategies.

In studies using the questionnaire, the goals toward which the self-regulatory behavior is directed are goals established by the instructor for the course and reflected in the assigned learning tasks which the student undertakes. The outcomes are typical teacher-created classroom achievement measures, and the processes of self-regulation are of primary interest. Thus, student goals are not assessed separately by the researchers. Additionally, no attempt is made in the Pintrich et al. model to examine course design or the academic plan used to generate the assigned learning tasks.

Students display a "positive" motivational orientation when they have high self-efficacy and low anxiety about a course, when they adopt a learning goal and effective learning strategies, and when they assign a high task value to a course. "Students who are generally active and self-regulating learners (e.g., high in cognitive and metacognitive activity including effort regulation) tend to be students who value, and are interested in, the course work" (Pintrich et al. 1988, p. 45). These students also believe they have high control regarding the tasks and hold high expectations of success.

Comparing students
Pintrich and associates describe "good" students as those who score high on all the expected aspects of classroom learning, and achieve well; "poor" students are those who achieve poorly. Three groups of "in-between" students achieve average grades. These include: students who are motivated to learn, but are not self- regulating in their study effort; students who are self-regulating but not motivated; and a third group

who are both self-regulating and motivated, but who do not expect to succeed.

Although its primary concern is with learning tasks, the work by McKeachie and Pintrich helps to spotlight the notion that students' course-related goals are more specific than the broad goals they bring to college. Course-level goals may contribute to student motivations and to the regulation of behavior. Still, intrinsic motivation (the student's interest in the task) may not be crucial to course success, relative to some other variables such as self-regulation (Pintrich et al. 1988, p. 50).

Student performance is a function of student goals interacting with variable properties of the immediate learning environment. "Variable properties"—such as course content, design, and instruction—can be manipulated to improve student effort and performance. For this reason, researchers such as Pintrich are working with discipline-specific learning tasks commonly offered in courses from diverse academic areas and with students actually enrolled in these courses, rather than in laboratory settings or with more general cognitive tasks.

How Important is Self-Efficacy?

Recently, the efforts of many researchers to understand human motivation have centered on social learning theory (Bandura 1982). The theory's proponents assert that interest and motivation are not static but grow when satisfaction is gained from fulfilling internal standards. Interest and motivation also grow when successful achievements increase an person's self-confidence in his/her ability to accomplish a task. In this theory, self-evaluation becomes extremely important in the process of setting goals. Self-efficacy can vary along a number of dimensions such as strength and specificity. For example, one can have a strong feeling of self-efficacy with respect to one's ability to dive, but a weak feeling with respect to playing the violin.

Inherent but not always stated in discussions of improving self-efficacy is the idea of establishing "do-able" goals and short-term goals that allow positive self-evaluation in a timely manner. Bandura describes rather clearly the relationship between goal dimensions and social learning theory.

Self-motivation is best summoned and sustained by adopting attainable subgoals that lead to large future ones. Whereas [short-term] proximal subgoals provide immediate

incentives and guides for action, distal [long-term] goals
are too far removed in time to effectively mobilize effort
or to direct what one does in the here and now. Proximal
goals can also serve as an important vehicle in the devel-
opment of self-percepts of efficacy. Without standards
against which to measure their performance, people have
little basis for judging how they are doing or for gauging
their capabilities. Subgoal attainments provide clear markers
of progress along the way to verify a growing sense of self-
efficacy" (Bandura 1982, p.134).

Bandura points out two ways that short-term goals can generate greater interest in an activity: Satisfaction based on goal
attainment can build intrinsic interest, and the sense of personal ability derived from achieving goals can spark interest
in a task. In short, in either diving or playing the violin, small
successes can lead to increased interest in practicing the skills.

A number of researchers, working at the level of learning
tasks, pursued those ideas. McKeachie et al. (1986) reviewed
their efforts in detail. This, however, assumes that success
alone will not motivate learning; the student also must have
a sense of control, or self-direction (Bandura 1982; Wittrock
1986). Like success, increased responsibility and control over
one's learning also leads to improved self-efficacy. This line
of argument assumes that if students are placed in carefully
structured learning environments which provide opportunities
for self-direction, their sense of their own abilities and personal control will be enhanced.

Some researchers are developing strategies for motivational
skills training (McCombs 1984). These are intended to
increase students' levels of self-efficacy and personal control
and, thus, to promote active participation in the learning
process.

Allowing people to create incentives for themselves, and
to enhance self-efficacy through successful goal attainment
is important (Bandura 1982). But, reciprocally, the increase
in self-efficacy may cause their goals to be strengthened.

In a related theory, causality is viewed as a separate issue
from control (Weiner 1985; 1986). In attribution theory, the
causes to which students attribute their successes and failures
affect their future expectations. Students who tend to attribute
success to their own abilities will expect to do well in the
future, whereas students who attribute success to external forces will not expect to do as well.

How to apply theories

Logical extensions of these ideas extend from cognitive science to curriculum and course design, but such extensions are not usually examined by psychological researchers. For example, with self-efficacy, an important potential extension may involve the relationship existing between attributing success and failure to goal setting in a course.

If students articulate course goals, it may be difficult for them to attribute the cause for failure elsewhere later. One may assume, in fact, that in assisting students to articulate course goals, faculty members might help them learn to attribute failure in ways that lead to future success.

A second extension occurs when teachers recognize students' course level goals and encourage students to act upon them. This may increase their ability to set new goals. Perhaps it is fair to say that in everyday conversation among college teachers, the term "active learning" includes, at the course and program level, the types of engagement, self-direction, improved self-efficacy, and conscious use of learning strategies with which psychologists are experimenting at the task level.

In laboratory models, psychologists examine relations between student achievement, self-efficacy, and motivation by focusing on a particular learning problem, say, solving a mathematical equation, or using literature to draw contrasts between historical events. Intrinsic interest (task value) likely will be higher, and meaningfulness increased, however, if this task is placed in its "natural domain," that is, in a course or academic program context that is viewed by the student as a meaningful link in educational progress.

Learning Styles

The study of learning styles is a popular area of research among educators. Since a person's learning style is applied toward some learning goal, a means-end relationship connects learning styles and goals. Drawn originally from personality trait theory, learning styles traditionally have been viewed as general dispositions used rather consistently in many life situations. For example, this is believed to be true of Witkin's field dependent and independent styles of thinking (Witkin, Moore, Goodenough, and Cox 1977). Recent concepts of "learning style," however, are not considered so rigid. For example, proponents of the Myers-Briggs Type Indicator, classifying learners as "sensers" and "intuitives," suggest that cer-

Teaching strategies relying heavily on extrinsic rewards can change students' goals and motivational patterns in directions that some consider undesirable.

tain teaching and counseling strategies can alter predispositions to behave in certain ways.

Another scheme, sometimes viewed as a learning style, but closely resembling some motivational orientations we have discussed, is the LOGO typology. The LOGO II, two-dimensional typology places students in four groups based on high or low scores on learning orientation (LO) and grade orientation (GO) (Eison, Pollio, and Milton 1982).

Learning orientation is defined as attitudes and behaviors based upon the view that college courses provide an opportunity to acquire knowledge and obtain personal enlightenment.

Grade orientation is defined as attitudes and behaviors based upon the view that the pursuit of course grades is a sufficient reason for being, and doing, in college.

A number of the 32-items in the LOGO II instrument resemble those used in scales purported to measure learning styles, learning strategies, or learning goals. Eison, Pollio, and Milton (1986) report that LOGO II correlates significantly with some other learning style instruments such as the Grasha-Reichmann Student Learning Style Survey (Reichmann and Grasha 1974), and the Inventory of Learning Processes (Schmeck, Ribich, and Ramanaiah 1977), but not with Kolb's Learning Style Inventory (1985). Some items are similar to those included in the Pintrich questionnaire. LOGO scores also are related to test anxiety and to study attitudes and skills.

Most relevant to this discussion is the possibility that grade or learning LOGO orientations can be changed (Milton, Pollio, and Eison 1986). In addition to intrinsic and extrinsic motivation as possible underlying bases for learning and grade orientations, the authors mention an "overjustification effect." Purportedly, this describes a situation in which the use of extrinsic rewards may interfere with, and undermine, the initial intrinsic gratification once produced by completing an activity (Eison, Pollio, and Milton 1982).

This implies that teaching strategies relying heavily on extrinsic rewards can change students' goals and motivational patterns in directions that some consider undesirable. If so, one may assume that other teaching strategies, perhaps based on sharing enthusiasm for certain learning goals, also could move students toward higher learning orientation scores on LOGO.

Another view of learning styles is related to student goals

in a somewhat different way. Kolb's experiential learning theory (1981) proposes that learners need four skills to be effective: concrete experience abilities, reflective observation, abstract conceptualization, and active experimentation.

The sets of skills represent two scales: active-reflective, and abstract-concrete. The learner uses immediate concrete observation to form the basis of a more abstract theory, which, in turn, serves as a guide for his or her behavior. Such a process seemingly affects the ability to set and achieve goals, break them into shorter-term goals, and then build upon success to adjust the next, broader goal.

Furthermore, based on results from his Learning Styles Inventory, Kolb classifies people into four learning-style types:

Convergers: Their dominant learning abilities are abstract conceptualization and active experimentation. They are strong in practical application of ideas.

Divergers: They are best at concrete experience and reflective observation. They also are strong in imaginative ability.

Assimilators: Their dominant learning abilities are abstract conceptualization and reflective observation. They also are strong in ability to create theoretical models.

Accommodators: They are best at concrete experience and active experimentation. Their greatest strength lies in the ability to carry out plans and experiments.

Kolb also classifies the disciplines to the extent that these learning styles are required in studying them. This classification suggests that students with certain learning styles will learn more effectively in certain types of disciplines, an assertion paralleling that of Holland's personality theory. Kolb found that persons whose disciplines (and associated learning styles) were incongruent with the dominant learning style of a specialized institution tended to feel isolated and confused.

At the institutional level, such incongruity might lead to lack of academic integration and eventual withdrawal, based more on incongruence of style rather than goals. At the course level, it might mean that a student possessing strong goal commitment toward a discipline, or having an important extrinsic need to study that academic subject nonetheless may feel out of place because of a discrepancy of learning styles. Recognizing whether the source of the discrepancy is goals or learning styles may be helpful in counseling students and facilitating learning.

Although Kolb's ideas are applicable to learning in personal, social, and vocational realms as well as academic realms, they seem to have special relevance at a time when considerable attention is being paid to introductory level general education courses. In the Kolb model, differentiating learning styles so they are consistent with specific disciplines or fields of endeavor is seen as development. For instance, when teaching introductory courses aimed at majors, students taking the course for general education purposes may have a poor success rate and a decrease in self-confidence. In the broadest terms, the result may be that general education reduces the student's motivation, self-efficacy, and tendency to set new goals for broadly-based liberal learning, rather than reinforcing positive motivational orientations. Clearly a college's view of whether to differentiate learning styles increasingly, or to make them more eclectic, is related to essential educational goals. It affects students' processes of goal revision as well.

Intellectual Development

Other developmental models, less closely allied with learning styles, also may be linked with goals and goal revision. Perry's scheme of intellectual growth (1970) is a popular developmental model based on empirical studies of college students over a number of years at Harvard. The model differs from others since it involves "positions" rather than "stages" of student development, and emphasizes the "transitions" between positions. The theory encompasses a dynamic view of growth, beginning with (1) dualism (views of good and bad based on authority), moving through (2) relativism (a multiplistic view), and progressing to (3) making a commitment to one's own view.

As students consider the same issues from an increasingly broader perspective, Perry describes their progress as a spiral rather than a straight line. Sometimes, too, students return to lower positions in the spiral. The progression, irregular but tending generally toward broader perspectives, resembles the self-regulating behavior ascribed to goals. New knowledge about one's self and one's performance continually results in adjustment of one's goals, just as new exposure to the world requires adjustment of one's world view. Perry implies that students' goals change with their intellectual development. When people change their way of looking at a particular subject or challenge, they change their way of approaching it as well. Without pursuing this point vigorously, the educator suggests that "further researches into cognitive and learning styles must include a consideration of the different meanings and purposes that the learners ascribe to learning in different contexts and at different times in their lives" (Perry 1981, p. 107). An interesting, and as yet unexplored, question is to analyze the types of goals students articulate to determine whether, subconsciously at least, they adopt goals likely to move them to the next transition in the Perry scheme.

Academic and Social Integration

Tinto offered a model of college attrition (1975) and later expanded it (1987). The model proposes that the process of deciding to leave college is similar to the decision to leave the world in suicide. The student who chooses to persist in college is more academically and socially integrated with the institution than the student who withdraws, just as the suicide victim often lacks integration with society. Seeing the relation of integration to goal fit requires little imagination. Beyond fit, however, Tinto's concept of integration seems to involve active engagement with key institutional processes of academic and social development. Although it is not usually considered in this way, Tinto's model resembles some popular classifications, particularly the Clark-Trow model, in the sense that it views a student as socially integrated, academically integrated, both, or neither.

Considerable research validating and extending Tinto's model led some college administrators to focus on academic and social integration as major institutional concerns. Quite possibly, however, student goals simultaneously affect which outcome (leaving or staying) results from integration. Just as researchers have included expectancies in frameworks describing goals, Tinto describes expectations as elements in the integration model. Goal commitment (strength), based on the expected value of attending college, and the student's self-efficacy can be viewed as the immediate precursor of dropping out. The student continually modifies goals and institutional commitments as experience causes self-assessment and self-regulation.

Tinto carefully points out that college "leavers" may see their action as a positive step toward goal fulfillment, particularly if their entry into college was not linked to degree completion. However, colleges desiring to retain students must integrate them into the social and intellectual fabric of the

institution, and doing so may require obtaining a valid picture of students who enter (Tinto 1987, pp. 180, 192).

Faculty-student relationship

The study of faculty-student interaction is partly an extension of Tinto's work, and partly a strand of research in its own right (Wilson et al. 1975). The logic supporting concern with this faculty-student relationship is that poor integration of students results either from insufficient interactions with others in the college, or from interactions that are insufficiently rewarding. Poor integration leads to low commitment and increases the probability of withdrawal.

Faculty-student interaction may supply the needed integration or rewarding relationship to sustain enrollment. It is relevant to our discussion that researchers measuring faculty-student interaction typically studied out-of-class interactions rather than interactions representing a meshing of the instructors' and students' learning goals. Yet, it is hard to imagine much informal out-of-class interaction occurring between students and their instructors if their basic educational goals differ greatly.

It is easy to extend Tinto's model to the academic program level, where dropping out might be characterized by changing majors, or the course level where, if drop-out is not possible, disengagement may occur. This parallelism argues for attention to student course-level goals to promote student-faculty interaction within the learning environment.

Pascarella and Chapman (1983) argue that Tinto's theory does not quite fit commuter students who have a social environment separate from the college. Since commuter students may lack a focus for social integration on campus, academic integration possibly is even more important and may center on the course or program level. In light of the multiple attributes of student goals at both the college and course level that emerge from theory, a great deal of original research on these issues remains to be done. Unfortunately, many studies are either secondary analyses or surveys in which the definition of goal commitment was limited to student responses to two items, highest expected degree and the importance of graduating from college.

Involvement in Learning

Some discussions connecting the retention of students, intellectual growth, and motivation for learning have encouraged educational institutions to convey a general intent to improve teaching and learning. For instance, the call to involve students in their learning. (NIE Study Group 1984; Astin 1984b). The level at which improvement is urged may vary (institutional, program, and classroom), and the terminology used supports a wide variety of changes: from assessing the success of colleges in promoting student achievement to the importance of integrating commuting students. "The effectiveness of any educational policy or practice is directly related to the capacity of that policy or practice to increase student involvement" (Astin 1984b, p. 306).

Yet, "student involvement" is a nebulous term, especially when applied to the increasingly diverse student population on today's campuses. The level of involvement necessary, and even how to measure this involvement, might change in moving from commuter students to adult students and on to a bewildering array of "special interest" student groups. It is important to remember that each student brings a unique set of goals and motivations to the classroom. These goals must be considered before determining what level and type of involvement is necessary for the student to improve his or her learning process.

For example, a part-time adult student who has returned to college to complete her bachelor's degree may have neither the time, nor the inclination to become involved in learning in the same way a traditional college student might. However, if institutional personnel can determine her goals, they can devise a type and level of involvement which will help increase her effort and achieve her goals. Perhaps, for example, such a student's involvement will be strengthened by faculty encouragement to apply newly learned skills in her off-campus job.

Although the mediating effect of student goals on effort and involvement is only speculative at this point, this relationship is well worth exploring.

Quality of Student Effort

Recent work by Pace (1984; 1987) focuses on students' retrospective reports of what types of intellectual, personal, and social growth opportunities they actually pursued while in college. We can view this "quality of effort" as a measure of what the student is putting into his or her own education, and thus as an inferred measure of the strength of goals. The implied cause and effect relationship here is in the opposite direction from the case in which students report their goals prior to college, thereby allowing predictions of their possible effort, success, or retention in school. Both directions deserve exploration.

- On the one hand, behavior is more likely to be active and purposeful if goals are clear and self-originated.

- On the other hand, Pace's assumption that students who report high quality of effort are strongly motivated seems to imply clear goals and other prerequisite capabilities and conditions helping to regulate their behavior.

Yet, either effort (Pace) or involvement (Astin) may be the manifestation, as well as the cause, of goal commitment.

Summary
A recent review (Terenzini 1987) classified studies of student development into two camps: those concerned with individual psychological aspects (such as studies of personality traits, or the stage theories of development); and those concerned with sociological determinations (asserting that much of student development is linked with environmental factors).

The psychological theories held sway in the early years of student development research and some forms of these theories still dominate. In general, however, research has not yet demonstrated such clear relationships between student development and environmental factors. For example, while some studies of African-American students on white campuses have shown that institutional factors affect student satisfaction (Peterson, Blackburn, Gamson et al. 1978), broader studies encompassing both a more general student population and broader environmental factors do not exist so far. Yet, better knowledge of student goals, especially when studied at the program and course level, may help us explore the links between societal factors and the development of goals, motivation, and achievement in the college setting.

COURSE-LEVEL GOALS: The Missing Link

Educators continue to measure student goals, primarily at the institutional level, with instruments that do not incorporate new knowledge about motivation, goal attributes, self-efficacy, and related items. Consequently, researchers cannot easily link the data collected to psychological or sociological concepts that might increase our understanding of student effort and learning in courses. The continued use of traditional goal measures does not increase the probability that colleges will use recently developed basic knowledge to improve instruction in the classroom.

What is the Case
for Course-Level Goals?

Currently, goals instruments usually are used for two very different purposes.

—At one extreme, goal surveys employ broad statements that provide general information about student intentions. Examples are: "I want to prepare for a life of meaningful participation in society," or "I want to have a successful career." Because of their breadth and social desirability, such statements frequently fail to discriminate meaningfully even between fairly distinct groups of students such as those likely to choose different majors. At best, these instruments are virtually useless as tools to assess and improve college teaching. At worst, critics claim their breadth leads to the development of crude student classifications with the potential for misuse. Such classification schemes tend to label students, rather than help them in achieving their plans.

—At the other extreme, research concerned primarily with how students establish learning goals focuses on specific academic tasks, often measuring student motivation toward such tasks, or describing behavior during particular learning activities. Examples include studies of the varied techniques students use in taking notes or in memorizing material in different ways.

Although knowledge of such behaviors helps psychologists advance basic understanding of human learning, faculty and administrators often ignore this research as irrelevant or too technical. Consequently, although focused on issues connected with actual learning, this research does not make much impact on the way instructors teach.

By emphasizing either broad college-level goals, or specific learning tasks, educators ignore course-level goals as a crucial

The continued use of traditional goal measures does not increase the probability that colleges will use recently developed basic knowledge to improve instruction in the classroom.

link in understanding how students and faculty members interact in educational settings. When the goals students bring to specific classes remain unexamined, it is difficult to identify factors that directly influence student course behavior and, reciprocally, to understand how courses may influence students' goals. In addition, since faculty members usually do not have measures of student course goals available, they cannot consider them when planning courses. As a result, instructors are unable to answer many crucial questions. For example:

- Which types of course-level goals lead to various kinds of student behavior?
- How do students' goals interact with the goals instructors incorporate into course plans?
- How are students' college-level goals translated into specific effort in the course context?
- Do different disciplines influence student goals in unique ways?
- To what extent, and in what circumstances, do students accept instructor's goals rather than direct their behavior toward their own goals?

Although the goals students bring to individual classes are neglected by educators, researchers, and administrators alike, knowledge of course goals is useful to each group as well as to students. Measures of course goals also are useful for the purposes given below.

1. As a way of assessing changes in the goals of a group of students over a semester or year within a specific course or program of study.

Example 1: As a result of course experiences, many instructors probably are interested in having students endorse more strongly a goal such as "to weigh and question the opinions of authorities." In some types of colleges with special missions, however, instructors might hope for weaker endorsement of this same statement.

2. As an element in programmatic or course-level assessment efforts.

Example 2: Achievement of student goals such as those which follow might be considered evidence of course or program success. At the course level, "to increase my self-confidence in public speaking." At the program level, "to prepare for a life of service to others."

3. As a mediating variable in studies linking student outcomes to desired course outcomes or to specific instructional strategies.

Example 3: We might expect desired outcomes to be achieved fairly readily when students enter a biology course with a goal such as "to develop keener awareness of my environment." We would not expect such quick success for those who first must be led to see the value of environmental awareness. In assessment, then, commitment to a goal, like student preparation, plays a part in learning success.

4. As a way to assist course instructors in understanding the goal patterns of students enrolled in their courses.

Example 4: In a required introductory course, it is likely that some students will endorse strongly a course goal such as "to enjoy works of art," while others do not have such a goal. Knowing something about the distribution of the desired goal among class members can help the instructor provide different motivations for different groups, thus providing individual instruction to become more effective.

5. As a communication device to help students understand their short- and long-range goals for a particular course, assess their own behavior in light of their goals, and expand their options.

Example 5: Assisting students to learn how to reflect on their own goals in learning can help them achieve the optimal amount of self-management. For instance, an instructor might help students recognize that short-term clinic or laboratory assignments have, as their ultimate aim, the achievement of longer-term goals such as "to appreciate individuality and independence in thought and action," or "to understand the way scholars ask questions."

Those potential uses of information about goals from specific courses are based on several assumptions that are supported by the literature reviewed in previous chapters. (1) The goals that students bring to a course, or program of study, influence their motivation to learn specific course material, their reaction to course activities, and the type and intensity of effort they exert in academic tasks. (2) Although goals change, the direction of change is not always the one desired by either teachers or students. (3) Goals are a crucial mediating variable when assessing the success of courses. (4) Goals can help instructors build upon student motivations and interest in course achievement.

The assumptions made above are integrated and related in figure 1. It represents a possible conceptualization of the relationships among college goals and course goals. In it, we assume that students' general college goals precede the goals they hold for a specific course. Students bring to college previous experiences that lead them to develop expectations about whether they need a specific course, whether they will enjoy it, and how well they will perform. At both college and course levels, we show the possible but untested influence of general motivating factors (such as expectations and self-assessment) as well as prior preparation. These issues are important at both levels because the self-confidence a student feels about college generally may not transfer to a specific course, nor is the preparation for a specific course the same as preparation for college generally.

FIGURE 1
General Framework for a Student Goals Inventory

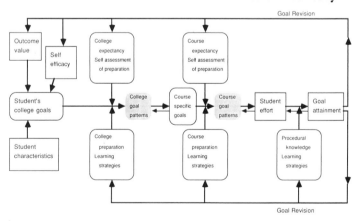

Note: Shaded boxes indicate hypothesized multidimensional patterns.

Therefore, while the combination of college and course goals is one known factor determining student effort for a course, other factors may include students' degree of self-confidence as learners, and their ability to use various learning strategies (McKeachie et al. 1986). This scheme assumes that students direct their effort toward course tasks, and, to some degree, attain results they, or their instructors, establish. Finally, it assumes that they revise both their self-assessments and their goals in light of new course experiences.

Many elements shown in the figure are measurable with existing instruments. For example, statements of general college goals used in the Cooperative Institutional Research Program (Astin, Green, and Korn 1987) are useful here. Another traditional measure, general college aptitude tests (SAT or ACT) can help to estimate actual preparedness for college. Similarly, the level of preparation for a given course can be judged either through area achievement tests provided by the same testing services, or by local placement tests.

Other figure parts require use of instruments that are more recent and still experimental. Pintrich's questionnaire (1988), for instance, provides items that assess course expectations, motivations, and learning strategies, along with some items concerned with assessing self-abilities and test anxiety. An instrument devised to assess the "quality of effort" students put into their college education as a whole (Pace 1987) may have potential for adaptation to effort at the course level.

In short, construction of a goal inventory for specific courses can benefit from existing instruments already constructed by psychologists and psychometricians concerned with related instuments. Further experimentation will identify useful items and their relationships.

Instruments are not currently available to measure two important parts of the conceptual scheme shown in figure 1.

—Except for general lists of results, there are few available lists of course-level goals that provide specificity at a level between the broad goal statements and the specific learning tasks studied by psychologists. It is promising that a number of researchers have begun to work almost simultaneously on this problem by talking with faculty or students about course-level goals and desired learning results (Cross, 1988a; Donald 1983; Stark, Lowther et al. 1988).

—Two boxes, termed "goal patterns," are shaded deliberately to imply that they are "fuzzy" concepts. We foresee that it is possible to construct multidimensional measures (both at the college and course level) to include the many goal attributes discussed: type, source, temporality, commitment, specificity. The possibility of devising a statistical "pattern profile," or "mapping," of both general types of student goals and their attributes has caused us to reserve the term "goal dimension" for such measures. For now, we use the word "pattern," acknowledging that the concepts in these boxes are not further developed.

Characteristics of a Course-Level Goals Inventory

1. *A course-level goals inventory should build upon learning theories and existing goal surveys.* Ideally, it should help us relate students' course-level goals to a) broad goals of college attendance, b) course motivation, c) course effort, and d) course achievement.

2. *It should include several dimensions of student goals.* Include those types of broad goals already well known—academic goals, personal goals, social goals, and vocational goals—in order to determine how they relate to newly measured goals specific to courses. But an inventory also should be sensitive to the specific characteristics of goals outlined in chapter 3 that can lead to a better understanding of goal patterns, especially source, specification, and temporality.

3. *A goals inventory for specific courses should not only be sensitive to specific content-embedded aspects of student goals; it should also incorporate essential dimensions of learning expected in varied disciplinary areas.* While the instrument should not focus totally on disciplinary content, its intellectual aspects nevertheless must account for the obvious differences that exist between disciplines. And yet, it still must be general enough to use in a variety of contexts.

4. *A goals inventory for specific courses should take into account what cognitive psychologists discovered about goal-setting and self-regulatory behavior.* To this end, the instrument should incorporate existing measures of motivation and self-efficacy which contribute to goal setting and goal revision. In this way, it will be possible to learn more

about students' feelings of control in a specific course.

While those guidelines is in no way complete, we believe that they provide a strong initial framework for constructing a course-level student goals inventory that will illuminate the currently fuzzy multidimensional patterns. However, we do not wish to imply that there is only one correct design for such an inventory. In fact, several designs come to mind.

In the next sections we will describe some frameworks that might guide the development of a goals inventory for specific courses. Each model would operate under a different set of assumptions, and given these assumptions, we will describe the broad approaches possible for a goals survey. Finally, we will describe a comprehensive model incorporating elements of each preceding model.

It is this combination model that currently guides our work to develop the "Student Goals Exploration," a course-level inventory we believe will prove useful to faculty members desiring to experiment with better understanding of student goals in their classes.

Possible Goal Inventory Models
Intellectual growth model
Although initially we criticized existing student goal instruments emphasizing intellectual goals as too broad to be useful, more specific intellectual goals are worthy of examination. Because of broad variations in how the disciplines contribute to a student's education, intellectual goals are most useful when examined at the course level.

That is, a goal such as "to improve my ability to analyze works of fiction" provides more helpful information than a response to a very broad college-level goal such as "to develop intellectually." Similarly, a goal such as "to increase my ability to persuade others" motivates better, at least in the short-term, than "to improve my communication skills."

The most effective courses are not defined wholly by either instructors' goals or students' goals. Instead, educators need to identify, and build upon, the common ground between their own goals and those of students. This process will make instructors more aware of student goals, and will assist students in developing a more focused set of goals appropriate to the academic field. Hence, the process of identifying goal statements to include on an inventory ideally involves both faculty and students.

The process of building a useful set of statements that tap intellectual goals of students in a course setting might begin by asking students to list intellectual goals for specific courses. Simultaneously, ask faculty what goals they hold for students as they teach courses. Faculty can do this readily, as evidenced by the more than 4,000 course goals they contributed to our Course Planning Exploration survey (Stark, Lowther et al., 1989).

Including goals mentioned by both faculty and students would enable us to determine whether, over time, students begin to adopt more discipline-specific goals modeled on those of their teachers. For example, as students progress through a core course in which human history is discussed in the context of the history of science, we would expect students to endorse more frequently a goal such as "to become aware of the consequences of new applications of science and technology." Such a specific goal might replace the more general goal "to learn more about science."

Making goal inventories powerful. A goals inventory based on the intellectual model could become considerably more powerful if the statements were written to represent varied levels of desired academic achievement. The levels of capability identified by Bloom (1956), for example, are particularly useful here because many faculty members are familiar with these hierarchical levels of learning, ranging from recognition to synthesis.

The difference between levels is illustrated by differing goal statements. For example, at a simple level of learning, students might set the goal "to read about a debate and recall some of the important points made on both sides of the argument." This is quite a different goal than "to synthesize literature about the question at issue and be able to debate both sides of the issue effectively." The responses to these goal items then could be analyzed by how well the specific goal matches the level of desired capability students achieve.

In a similar way, researchers could assess student goals by including statements representing various levels of intellectual development based on Perry's scheme. Goals such as "to understand specific facts in this field," "to become aware of different philosophies, cultures and ways of life," and "to be able to appreciate the individuality of others," arguably represent different positions in Perry's scheme of intellectual growth.

Of course, other intellectual development scales, such as Kolb's, also could be used. The purpose of a goals inventory is not to try and demonstrate that students do, or do not, have the "correct" goals for courses, but, instead, to recognize and promote the meshing of student and instructor goals.

Summary. We do not wish to imply that any one theoretical scheme is superior to any other. It is important, however, to use some organizing framework to encompass adequately, and to interpret, the range of intellectual goals students and faculty might aspire to. It also is important to suggest appropriate items. The diversity of courses, instructors, and institutions precludes "quick and dirty" construction of goals inventories.

Regardless of the specific framework chosen, faculty should share it with students as they try to help them set goals more effectively and realistically.

Personal and social development model
Personal and social goal statements are prominent in existing college-level goals inventories. Broad examples of such statements are "I wanted to go to college because my friends were going," and "I wanted to get away from home." Research also confirms that such goals are important to students.

Although some faculty believe that such goals are inappropriate for the classroom, others believe that both faculty and students deliberately should seek achievement of personal and social goals. This is particularly true for instructors of literature, sociology, and similar fields (Stark et al. 1988a).

Statements reflecting both personal and social goals that students hope to achieve in a course, and those that faculty hope to cultivate, could be collected in a manner similar to that suggested for the intellectual goals model. But the organizing framework should differ. For example, researchers could use concentric circles to portray the importance of gaining an increasingly broader view of the world.

The smallest (most central) circle contains the most personal goals (for example, "to develop new friendships").

Moving outward, goals include the desire to recognize, or appreciate, the diverse views of others (for example, "to learn to get along with different kinds of people").

The outermost circle could characterize a goal of international, or global, understanding (for example, "to work for the cause of international peace").

Viewed in this way, social and personal goals are appropriately the province of academic courses. Such frameworks allow educators to test the hypothesis that as students move through these successively more encompassing circles over time, they will endorse goals that gradually become less egocentric and more directed at others.

Vocational development model

Students appear increasingly vocational in recent years, a trend that concerns college educators and the public alike. Students characterize vocational orientations most frequently as "I want to get a better job after college," or "I want to be well-off financially." Paradoxically, students entering college without a distinct career in mind often are characterized as lacking maturity because they have not made a career decision. Without a career orientation, their chances of dropping out are higher (Gordon 1984, p. 4). Examining the vocational goals that students bring to particular classes could shed much light on the conceptual confusion evident in this paradox.

An extensive literature on vocational education points to a fundamental difference between "exploratory" and "preparatory" vocational goals. Since it is possible to characterize vocational aspirations at these different levels, students appropriately might have vocational goals of two types, at least. To include both, then, an instrument might include goal items focusing on appropriate explorations of career choice. For example, "to understand my own interests in relation to this course," or "to explore the possibility of becoming a nurse." It also could include more specific goal items concerned with developing skills and knowledge to enable the student to enter a previously selected career. For example, "to succeed in a business course," or "to understand sufficient biology for a career in nursing."

Well-known career maturity inventories may provide a model for appropriate goal statements concerning the career exploration and decision process. Career development literature attributes several "deficiencies" to students "undecided" about their vocation. Restating these so-called "deficits" as legitimate goals for students could help researchers determine whether, and where, each operates. For example, since the literature identifies a lack of independence in decision making as a barrier to developing sound vocational goals, a goal statement such as "to gain independence in decision making" would enable us to identify those students who perceive a lack in their vocational development to date. Such goals statements would illuminate vocational development in a way that context-free vocational goal statements cannot.

Specific statements concerned with career development may be based on statements from specialized accrediting agencies and professional associations. In addition, statements

The most effective way to improve our understanding of student goals, therefore, may lie in examining several goal attributes simultaneously.

on results generated by faculty in undergraduate professional fields such as nursing also could help the thoughtful researcher construct a course-specific vocational goals instrument. Such outcomes as "the ability to integrate theory and practice in professional activities," or "to understand the context in which the profession will be practiced," are relevant general goals for vocationally-oriented students. However, students may not articulate them independently (Stark, Lowther, and Hagerty 1986). Of course, statements contributed by students should be included as well.

Learner development model
For some years, agencies such as the College Board and the American College Testing Service have found that many pre-college students recognize their lack of preparedness for college work and report a need for assistance with specific subjects and basic learning strategies. Instructors recognize lack of preparedness too. A recent study found that only five percent of the faculty teaching introductory courses thought students were well prepared, while almost 19 percent thought they were "not at all" prepared (Stark et al. 1989). Yet faculty do not link this lack of preparedness with a lack of student effort; only 11.5 percent of those surveyed reported relatively little effort on the part of students. Clearly, the relationship between preparedness, goals, and effort has not been explored fully at the course level.

Pintrich (1988) developed some definitions of preparedness based on four dimensions: motivation, self-concept, possession of basic skills, and possession of study skills. He also related motivation to the self-assessment of abilities and test anxiety. Pintrich and others now are demonstrating in classroom settings that students can be helped to become more deliberate in trying to improve their learning strategies. Materials supporting classroom use of Pintrich's questionnaire will be available in a manual tentatively titled "Teaching Tips for the MSLQ."

Inventory models that also identify students' desire to increase learning skills and self-assessment of abilities well may improve their processes of self-regulatory behavior by raising their level of consciousness about them. In addition, by comparing a student's responses to surveys to subsequent class performance, such an inventory can help determine the level of realism that students possess and suggest corrective action.

Multidimensional model

While any of the four models outlined above would increase significantly our scanty knowledge about student goals and their utility, each has strengths and weaknesses. By combining elements of these models, perhaps we can arrive at a more comprehensive picture of the multidimensional goal "patterns" students bring to college and to the classroom. Goal patterns attempt to measure identifiable goal attributes and orientations about motivations connected to a specific course.

Understandably, educators prefer typologies that they can represent simply, such as in two-by-two dimensional tables. But, since goals have multiple attributes, attempting to develop measures of even three important goal attributes can provide considerably more explanatory power about goals.

College and course goals interact in important ways with other variables. In the same way, the concept of extrinsic and intrinsic motivation, based on the expected value of goal outcomes, also can serve to increase understanding of student goals if we look at their interaction with other dimensions. The most effective way to improve our understanding of student goals, therefore, may lie in examining several goal attributes simultaneously. Perhaps we should think of goal attributes and domains as acting jointly to satisfy both short-term goals and relatively long-range goals.

For example, considering goal specificity, source, and time span allows researchers eight potential ways to describe student goals. This invites richer interpretations than a two-way typology yielding four descriptions. Adding goal domains (vocational, social, academic and personal), type of motivation associated with the goal (intrinsic or extrinsic), and a measure of goal commitment results in an extremely complex but more sophisticated set of possibilities. Because of their complexity, multidimensional goal patterns might be portrayed best in more flexible formats (such as a vector or profile) rather than as a typology. Techniques such as those described by Cole and Hanson (1971), and used by Stern in mapping college environments (1970) possibly are good models for this task.

Until a statistical profile of the relationships between these dimensions is available, our mental processes may limit us to comprehending only two or three dimensions at a time. Nevertheless, it is intriguing to speculate on how various combinations of goal dimensions may illuminate dilemmas left unresolved by simpler classifications.

For example, consider the students Katchadourian and Boli (1985) called the "Unconnecteds." They, apparently, are interested in neither a good education nor a career. Within the group, however, considering goals in terms of source (parents), time span (short-term), and commitment, we can identify three very different sub-groups:

Rebels, chafing under imposed parental goals that they attend college, possibly in opposition to their own long-range goals;

Floaters, possessing weak educational goals or strong competing goals;

Dutifuls, pursuing short-term goals, with a "hard work" ethic or "sense of duty" deeply ingrained by their families, and seemingly the opposites of the "rebels."

Such conceptions are useful because they have the potential to solve the puzzle of the composition of the "nonconformist," or "unconnected," groups that appear in every empirically derived typology.

Unquestionably, there is an important trade-off between achieving better understanding of goals through using several dimensions, and the need for simple displays that help faculty adjust instructional methods. Balancing the two needs is a challenging problem. However, before we can portray our knowledge, it is important to have a firm idea of what we are portraying. The more comprehensive student goals model suggested here, then, represents this necessary first step.

How a Goals Inventory
Improves Teaching and Learning

Would instructors use the information gained from administering a course-related student goals inventory in their classes if one were available? While some might not, we believe that many would use it, based on findings that student preparation, self-confidence, and goals are important to faculty as they plan most introductory courses (Stark et al. 1988).

The same studies tell us that faculty teaching in some fields (literature) are far more likely to use measures of student goals than faculty in other fields (mathematics). We cannot concur with skeptics who view all faculty as resistant to any new ideas about improving teaching.

Only modest gains in teaching improvement would result if researchers administered goals inventories and provided the results to faculty members. Greater gains could be expected if faculty were involved in helping use a goals inventory in their classrooms, perhaps adding some goals they feel are particularly important. This involvement would promote instructors' increased awareness of their own teaching goals and the learning goals of their students. Raised awareness also might encourage faculty members to discuss course goals more frequently with students, thus fostering self-direction and active learning in students.

On another level, faculty are likely to become more interested in helping students achieve important goals such as independent thinking since part of this valued educational outcome is the ability to generate and pursue increasingly specific and enduring goals.

Classroom research and its status
The idea of classroom research to improve teaching and learning is taking root rapidly in many institutions. A researcher, convinced "that assessment is taking place too far from the scene of the action," supports "small-scale assessments conducted continuously in college classrooms by discipline-based teachers . . . . " (Cross 1986a, p. 29). She says this is necessary if the ultimate goal of assessment is instructional improvement based on the actions of teachers.

Faculty, responding to that appealing notion, are using varied techniques to determine how their teaching is going and how students are reacting to it (Cross and Angelo 1988). Because the intent and process of determining course level goals are similar to some classroom research techniques, the current receptive climate makes it an optimum time to begin to measure student goals and to assess their continued development.

An important concept emerging in learning improvement is "metacognition," the self-observation and self-monitoring of the learning process by the learner. Since good learners are more conscious of their learning processes (Cross 1988, p. 26; McKeachie et al. 1986), helping students to articulate their goals helps them to monitor their learning processes as well. Since the process of establishing revised goals is often a transfer of control from external sources to the student, students increasingly can control their learning process.

The recent emergence of such ideas suggests a proliferation of studies on course goals. However, such research, curiously, is absent from the literature. To our knowledge, there are no such studies of student goals.

Using a Goals Inventory in Assessment

How would measuring course-level student goals help improve assessment processes? College faculty and administrators heatedly debate a wide variety of assessment measures and motivations. Much of the controversy centers on who decides what to measure, and who uses the results to bring about change. (See Alexander and Stark 1986 for a fuller discussion.)

Setting those controversies aside for the moment, we concentrate here on the *technical* side of assessment to illustrate how student goal measures might become part of the picture.

Technically, it is possible to consider three procedures representing increasingly complex levels in assessing results.

1. The first level merely describes the degree to which students possess a particular capability, or characteristic.

The description provides a simple frequency distribution showing student characteristics using percentages, means, or raw scores. Instructors easily can construct such descriptions.

2. The next level, commonly known as "value-added," uses measures at two points in time to show whether, and how, the student has changed.

Recently, many colleges have begun to measure and illustrate these changes over time by subtracting student scores on some measure at "time one" from the scores at "time two." Usually, administrative or research offices make these measurements, using some type of standardized test. Even in capable hands, however, this technique has considerable potential for error in interpretation. (For good discussions of statistical and interpretation problems, see MacMillan 1988, Hanson 1988.)

Classroom instructors who are not psychometricians should proceed with caution. Classes already possessing a capability, by definition, cannot show much "value added." Furthermore, some students may gain capabilities while others lose, resulting in an apparent finding of no difference.

3. At the most complex level, an assessment process measures changes in students' scores, and also attempts to attribute these changes to the educational process.

The process is complex because it requires statistical adjustment for preexisting variations among students, and the ability to rule out possible sources of student change other than the course, or college, experience. The most common illustration includes studies in which end of term scores are regressed on student entry characteristics (or beginning of term scores) to provide statistical control of entry level variations. Then the differences between the expected and observed scores (regression residuals) are used as the measure of change (dependent variable). Clearly, such procedures require a competent statistician.

Using either of the simpler (but less comprehensive) statistical procedures allows researchers to compare groups of students who hold different scores on a goals inventory. In interpreting the data, however, they are limited to comparing a relatively small number of groups differing initially on one or two goal dimensions.

The third, more complex procedure could use measures of numerous dimensions of goals as additional variables in the statistical process. This would make any comparison of student groups more meaningful by taking into account their initial goals in the same way that their age, prior test scores, or gender are controlled statistically.

Of course, many instructors would need statistical help with such a procedure. Therefore, there is an important trade-off between classroom research that instructors can do privately and simply, and the greater accuracy and precision of the third method.

Finally, since goal change is a developmental activity, changes in goal measures can become dependent variables in a longitudinal change design. Preferably, researchers could examine such goal change by the more complex, statistical procedure of examining the residuals of postcourse goals regressed upon initial goals.

Administrative Uses of Goals Inventory

Administrators commonly collect general goals as students enter college, but they seldom attempt to collect finer grained descriptions of student goals. If more detail were available, however, administrators could use information about goals to guide students with certain goal patterns to certain advisors, certain educational experiences, and certain college services.

Particular decisions made on the basis of student goals will depend on local factors. Students need to experience some challenging, but not too challenging, situations as they seek to implement, develop, and clarify their goals. Finally, examining student goals may increase administrative awareness of the complexity, and potentially undesirable, aspects of some assessment models that ignore student goals and characteristics.

Developing a Course Goals Inventory
It is appropriate at this point to share, briefly, some ideas that have emerged during the initial process of collecting goal items for our course specific goals inventory and testing them with about 3,000 students in numerous introductory courses at three universities.

We believe that faculty will be surprised, concerned, and motivated to take action when they discover how narrowly conceived most student goals are for courses. Many opportunities exist for improved communication if faculty want students to recognize even a few of the goals they hope students will achieve.

To illustrate some of the differences in views between faculty and students, students see problem-solving as pertinent primarily in mathematics courses; faculty see it as a goal in most courses.

In some required introductory courses, where students have had little secondary school background (for example, fine arts courses), it appears that many students may enter college classes without any course-related goals in mind at all.

Although it may not come as a surprise that students' goals for courses often relate to the usefulness of the material in life and work, instructors may wish to seek ways to build on these strong extrinsic motivations to make course material come alive for students.

As those simple illustrations show, use of a student goals inventory, even in the simplest way, can help faculty members assist students in framing relevant goals and in striving toward the goals they already hold.

It appears possible to construct short scales that can distinguish among students enrolled in several introductory courses. We expect these scales will be more distinctive (because of stronger goals) for upperclass students majoring in each field.

An interesting, and open, question is whether students tend to broaden or narrow their goals with respect to specific areas of study as they proceed through their college years.

1. Do students who take more courses in a subject develop broader goals for the application of that field, or more specific goals?
2. Do their goals become clearer?
3. Are they more likely to be self-originated goals?
4. With the new emphasis on core courses, particularly interdisciplinary ones, will students taking these courses have broad goals when they begin these courses?
5. Will students in core courses change their goals in different ways from those of students who are fulfilling distribution requirements?

In our trials of potential course-related items, we noted that students perhaps are less likely than faculty to expect personal and social goals to be fulfilled in their classes. This fairly clear separation of the intellect from other life aspects is not desired by faculty members who believe personal enrichment is a goal of their classes. Nor is it desired by colleges which view value clarification as an important mission.

Scholars of higher education, campus institutional researchers and faculty members who share an interest in classroom research and teaching improvement will find numerous questions to examine from a data base of goals for specific courses.

Although we have not yet pursued them with a representative sample of student responses, we are curious about the relation of course-related goals to gender, ethnic group, and socioeconomic background. Many other questions come to mind too.

For example: Will students who acquire an increased sense of self-efficacy based on success in courses revise their self-image and goals in all courses, or only in specific courses? In which courses do students who otherwise apparently are drifting without clear educational goals get excited about learning? What causes such effects? Are there course-related goals that are linked with current theories of student attrition from college?

Conclusion

In the early 1970s, some researchers concluded that the impact of the college classroom upon students was minor "insofar as any changes in (student) value systems, character, or general social behavior are concerned" (Kees and McDougall 1971). Others concluded that it is impossible to determine the academic impact of college beyond what is attributable to characteristics students bring with them.

Such assertions discouraged meaningful research about the classroom environment for nearly two decades while studies of students in social settings and dormitories predominated. As a result, proposals for learning reforms in the mid-1980s were weakened by a dearth of knowledge about the academic side of campus life.

Yet, assertions that the classroom impact is minor and that the impact of college defies measurement perhaps were premature. Researchers now urge that these same questions be examined again at an organizational level closer to the student's daily academic life.

New knowledge indicates that perhaps the academic and personal-social areas were separated too sharply, and that the relations among attitudes, goals, and motivation for learning deserve a second look. We propose that the appropriate lower level of academic environment for this exploration is the course.

APPENDIX

A-1

BROAD GOAL ITEMS IN MAJOR SURVEYS

From Cooperative Institutional Research Program

In deciding to go to college, how important to you was each of the following reasons?

To be able to get a better job
To gain a general education and appreciation of ideas
To improve my reading and study skills
There was nothing better to do
To make me a more cultured person
To make more money
To learn more about things that interest me
To prepare myself for graduate or professional school
My parents wanted me to go
I could not find a job
Wanted to get away from home

Indicate the importance to you personally of each of the following:

Becoming accomplished in one of the performing arts (acting, dancing, etc.)
Becoming an authority in my field
Obtaining recognition from my colleagues for contributions to my special field
Influencing the political structure
Influencing social values
Raising a family
Having administrative responsibility for the work of others
Being very well off financially
Helping others who are in difficulty
Making a theoretical contribution to science
Writing original works (poems, novels, short stories, etc.)
Creating artistic work (painting, sculptures, decorating, etc.)
Being successful in a business of my own
Becoming involved in programs to clean up the environment
Developing a meaningful philosophy of life
Participating in a community action program
Helping to promote racial understanding
Becoming an expert on finance and commerce

Source: Astin et al, 1986.

A-2

BROAD GOAL ITEMS IN MAJOR SURVEYS

From Educational Testing Service

1. My main goal in college will be to get training for the work I want to do, or make the grades I need to get into a good school after I finish here.

2. I see college as my great opportunity to read a lot, exchange ideas, learn about the significant cultures of the world, and generally to become an aware and more sophisticated person.

3. I'm an active person. I like sports and other outdoor activities. Developing my talents and interests in this area is important to me.

4. I view college as a place where a person can learn practical skills valuable through a lifetime. I am especially interested in developing specific skills such as foreign language competency, computer programming, reading and math skills, good work habits, etc.

5. I don't want to just learn a lot of facts in college. To me it's very important to learn how to deal with those facts. For example, learning how to reason, evaluate information, and construct a defensible argument are high priorities for me.

6. Extra curricular activities appeal to me because they are a good way to get a lot out of your education; especially learning how to organize resources, work with others, and take the lead in achieving an objective. I hope to participate fully in this aspect of college life.

7. I am not at all sure what I want to do for a career. To me it seems important that I get a better sense of direction, and I hope to do that in college.

8. I am especially concerned about ethical, moral and religious issues. In the next year or so I would like to get a better sense of my own values in this area.

9. I would very much like to develope a meaningful relationship with another person while I'm in college. If it's lasting, good. If it's not, that's OK too.

10. I like to express myself creatively. I already have some talent in an area of interest to me (for example, theater, music, painting, crafts, writing), and want to develop it further in college.

11. I am very interested in community and social problems and would like to learn more about what's going on in the world. The opportunity to get personally involved in some sort of significant community service activity or environmental project would be important to me.

12. In the next few years, I would like particularly to develop more skill and confidence in dealing with different kinds of people. I think the social side of college is very important.

Source: Willingham, 1985.

A-3
BROAD GOAL ITEMS IN MAJOR SURVEYS

From Questionnaire on Student and College Characteristics

College students have different ideas about the purpose of a college education, some of which are listed below. As you read this list, consider what goals are important to you. Mark the goal that is *most* important to you, and the goal that is *second most important*. Also mark your *least important* college goal.

To broaden my intellectual interests and to acquire an appreciation of ideas

To increase my appreciation of art, music, and literature

To decide upon an occupation or career and develop the necessary skills

To increase my effectiveness in working with people and in getting along with different kinds of people

To develop my knowledge and interest in community and world problems

To help clarify my moral and ethical values

To acquire knowledge and attitudes basic to marriage and a satisfying family life

To acquire background for further study in some professional or scholarly field

Source: Centra 1970.

A-4
BROAD GOAL ITEMS IN MAJOR SURVEYS

From NCHEMS/College Board Student Outcomes Questionnaire Entering Student Version — Two Year Institutions

The following statements reflect the goals of many college students. Please circle the letters of all those goals that are important to you.

Academic goals

A. To increase my knowledge and understanding in an academic field

B. To obtain a certificate or degree

C. To complete courses necessary to transfer to another educational institution

D. Other _____

Career Preparation Goals

E. To discover my career interests
F. To formulate long-term career plans and/or goals
G. To prepare for a new career
H. Other _____

Job or Career-Improvement Goals

I. To improve my knowledge, technical shills, and/or competencies required for mu job or career
J. To increase my chances for a raise and/or promotion
K. Other _____

Social and Cultural Participation Goals

L. To become actively involved in student life and campus activities
M. To increase my participation in cultural and social events
N. To meet people
O. Other _____

Personal-Development and Enrichment Goals

P. To increase my self-confidence
Q. To improve my leadership skills
R. To learn skills that will enrich my daily life or make me a more complete person
S. To develop my ability to be independent, self-reliant, and adaptable
T. Other _____

Source: The National Center for Higher Education Management Systems and The College Board 1983.

A-5

DETAILS OF SOME COMMON TYPOLOGIES

Feldman and Newcomb (1969)

Professionalist, Activist, Disaffiliate, Big Man on Campus, Apprentice, Underachiever, and Gentleman-in-waiting.

Educational Testing Service (1965, College Student Questionnaires)

Philosophy A This philosophy emphasizes education essentially as preparation for an occupational future. Social or purely intellectual phases of campus life are relatively less important, although certainly not ignored. Concern with extracurricular activities and college traditions is relatively small. Persons holding this philosophy are usually quite committed to particular fields of study and are in college primarily to obtain training for careers in their chosen fields.

Philosophy B This philosophy, while it does not ignore career preparation, assigns greatest importance to scholarly pursuit of knowledge and understanding, wherever the pursuit may lead. It entails serious involvement in course work or independent study beyond the minimum required. Social life and organized extracurricular activities are relatively unimportant. Thus, while others aspects of college life are not to be forsaken, this philosophy attaches greatest importance to interest in ideas, pursuit of knowledge, and cultivation of the intellect.

Philosophy C This philosophy holds that, besides occupational training and/or scholarly endeavor, an important part of college life exists outside the classroom, laboratory, and library. Extracurricular activities, living-group functions, athletics, social life, rewarding friendships, and loyalty to college traditions are important elements in one's college experience and necessary to the cultivation of the well-rounded person. Thus, while not excluding academic activities, this philosophy emphasizes the importance of the extracurricular side of college life.

Philosophy D This philosophy is held by the student who either consciously rejects commonly held value orientations in favor of his own, or who has not really decided what is to be valued and is in a sense searching for meaning in life. There is often deep involvement with ideas and art forms both in the classroom and in sources (often highly original and individualistic) in the wider society. There is little interest in business or professional careers; in fact there may be a definite rejection of this kind of aspiration. Many facets of the college-organized extracurricular activities, athletics, traditions, the college administration, are ignored or viewed with disdain. In short, this philosophy may emphasize individualistic interests and styles, concern for personal identity and often, contempt for many aspects of organized society.

Holland (1966, 1985)

Realistic Type The realistic person prefers activities that entail the explicit, ordered, or systematic manipulation of objects, tools, machines, and animals, and has an aversion to educational or therapeutic activities. These behavioral tendencies lead in turn to the acquisition of competencies and to a deficit in social and educational competencies.

Investigative Type The investigative person prefers activities that entail the observational, symbolic, systematic, and creative investigation of physical, biological, and cultural phenomena in order to understand and control such phenomena; and has an aversion to persuasive, social, and repetitive activities. These behavioral tendencies lead in turn to an acquisition of scientific and mathematical competencies and to a deficit in persuasive competencies.

Artistic Type The Artistic person prefers ambiguous, free, unsystematic activities that entail the manipulation of physical, verbal or human material to create art forms or products, and has an aversion to explicit, tendencies lead, in turn, to an acquisition of artistic competencies in language, art, music, drama, writing—and to a deficit in clerical or business system competencies.

Social Type The social person prefers activities that entail the manipulation of others to inform, train, develop, cure or enlighten, and has an aversion to explicit, ordered, systematic activities involving materials, tools, or machines. These behavioral tendencies lead in turn to an acquisition of human relations competencies such as interpersonal and education competencies, and to a deficit in manual and technical competencies.

Enterprising Type The enterprising person prefers activities that entail the manipulation of others to attain organizational goals or economic gain, and has an aversion to observational, symbolic, and systematic activities. These behavioral tendencies lead in turn to an acquisition of leadership, interpersonal, and persuasive competencies, and to a deficit in scientific competencies.

Conventional Type The conventional person prefers activities that entail the explicit, ordered, systematic manipulation of data, such as keeping records, filing materials, reproducing materials, organizing written and numerical data according to a prescribed plan, operating business machines and data processing machines to attain organizational or economic goals. He or she has an aversion to ambiguous, free, exploratory, or unsystematized activities. These behavioral tendencies lead in turn to an acquisition of clerical, computational, and business system competencies and to a deficit in artistic competencies.

Hackman and Taber (1979)

Successful Students Leaders, scholars, careerists, grinds, artists, athletes, and socializers.

Unsuccessful Students Disliked, extreme grinds, alienated, unqualified, and directionless.

College Student Questionnaires, Educational Testing Service (1968, revised 1971)

Family Independence refers to a generalized autonomy in relation to parents and parental family. Students with high scores tend to perceive themselves as coming from families that are not closely united, as not consulting with parents about important personal matters, as not concerned about living up to parental expectations, and the like. Low scores suggest "psychological" dependence on parents and family.

Peer Independence refers to a generalized autonomy in relation to peers. Students with high scores tend not to be concerned about how their behavior appears to other students, nor to consult with acquaintances about personal matters, and the like. They might be thought of as unsociable, introverted, or inner-directed. Low scores suggest conformity to prevailing peer norms, sociability, extraversion, or other-directedness.

Liberalism is defined as a political-economic-social value dimension, the nucleus of which is sympathy either for an ideology of change or for an ideology of preservation. Students with high scores (liberals) support welfare state activities, organized labor, abolition of capital punishment, and the like. Low scores (conservatism) indicate opposition to welfare legislation, to tampering with the free enterprise system, to persons disagreeing with American political institutions, etc.

Social Conscience is defined as moral concern about perceived social injustice and what might be called "institutional wrongdoing" (as in government, business, unions). High scores express concern about poverty, illegitimacy, juvenile crime, materialism, unethical business and labor union practices, graft in government, and the like.

Cultural Sophistication refers to an authentic sensibility to ideas and art forms, a sensibility that has developed through knowledge and experience. Students with high scores report interest in, or pleasure from, such things as wide reading, modern art, poetry, classical music, discussions of philosophies of history, and so forth. Low scores indicate a lack of cultivated sensibility in the general area of the humanities.

Motivated for Grades refers to a relatively strong desire—retrospectively reported—to earn good marks in secondary school. High scores represent the respondent's belief that others (e.g., teachers, classmates) regarded him or her as a hard worker, that the respondent, in his or her estimation, studies extensively and efficiently, was capable of perseverance in school assignments, and considered good grades to be personally important. Low scores indicate lack of concern for high marks in secondary school.

Family Social Status is a measure of the socioeconomic status of the respondent's parental family. The scale has four questions, each having nine scaled alternatives. The four items have to do with: fathers's occupation, fathers's education, mother's education, and family income. Father's occupation is given the weight of three.

Sheldon and Grafton (1982)

Community college students include full-time transfers, part-time transfers, the undisciplined transfers, the technical transfers, the intercollegiate athletes, the financial support seekers, the expediters and program completers, the job seekers, the job upgraders, the career changers, the licence maintainers, the leisure-skill students, the education seekers, the art and culture students, the explorer/experimenters, the basic skills students, and the lateral transfers.

Katchadourian and Boli (1985)

Intellectuals: College is a place where they can broaden their established academic interests, develop their intellectual capabilities, and seek out new interests and challenges. They are less concerned about preparing for professional careers...what sets them apart is neither the power of their intellect nor their social lifestyle, but their attitude toward intellectual issues.

Careerists: For careerists, the choice of academic major largely turns on one question: Which major will best prepare me for my chosen career? There are two forms this concern can take. The first is to choose a major that equips one for immediate employment upon graduation, without the necessity of further schooling. The alternative route is to use the major as preparation for further professional studies.

Strivers: Strivers want a good education and a good job. That statement neatly sums up the orientation of students in this group. Like intellectuals, they value liberal education. Like careerists, they are concerned about successful careers.

Unconnected: These are students who fail to engage fully in their college education for no obvious reasons. They appear to be rel-

atively indifferent to both career preparation and liberal education
. . . being unconnected is not an academic orientation in the same
sense that being a careerist, intellectual, or striver is. They form a
composite picture with a common theme but distinctive and often
unrelated variations. There are many ways and many reasons for
being unconnected.

Source: Bomotti, May 1987.

REFERENCES

The Educational Resources Information Center (ERIC) Clearinghouse
on Higher Education abstracts and indexes the current literature on
higher education for inclusion in ERIC's data base and announce-
ment in ERIC's monthly bibliographic journal, *Resources in Education* (RIE). Most of these publications are available through the
ERIC Document Reproduction Service (EDRS). For publications cited
in this bibliography that are available from EDRS, ordering number
and price code are included. Readers who wish to order a publication should write to the ERIC Document Reproduction Service,
3900 Wheeler Avenue, Alexandria, Virginia 22304. (Phone orders
with VISA or MasterCard are taken at 800/227-ERIC or 703/823-0500.)
When ordering, please specify the document (ED) number. Doc-
uments are available as noted in microfiche (MF) and paper copy
(PC). If you have the price code ready when you call EDRS, an exact
price can be quoted. The last page of the latest issue of *Resources
in Education* also has the current cost, listed by code.

Abe, C., and Holland, J. L. 1965. *A Description of College Freshman:
Students with Different Vocational Choices.* ACT Research Report
No. 4. Iowa City, Iowa: American College Testing Program.

Adelman, C. August 1984. *Starting with Students: Promising
Approaches in American Higher Education.* Washington, D.C.: U.S.
Government Printing Office.

Adelman, C., ed. 1988. *Performance and Judgment: Essays on Prin-
ciples and Practice in the Assessment of College Student Learning.*
Washington, D.C.: U.S. Department of Education, Office of Educational Research and Improvement.

Aitken, N. 1982. "College Student Performance, Satisfaction, and
Retention: Specification and Estimation of a Structural Model."
Journal of Higher Education 53(1): 32–50.

Alexander, J., and Stark, J. 1986. *Focusing on Student Outcomes: A
Working Paper.* Ann Arbor, Mich.: University of Michigan, National
Center for Research to Improve Postsecondary Teaching and
Learning.

American Association of State Colleges and Universities. 1986. *To
Secure the Blessings of Liberty: Report of the National Commission
on the Role and Future of State Colleges and Universities.* Washington, D.C.: American Association of State Colleges and
Universities.

Association of American Colleges. 1985. *Integrity in the College Curriculum. Washington, D.C.: Association of American Colleges.*

Astin, A. W. 1978. *Four Critical Years: Effects of College on Belief,
Attitudes, and Knowledge.* San Francisco: Jossey-Bass.

———. May 1982. "The American Freshman, 1966-1981: Some Implications for Educational Policy and Practice." Washington, D.C.:
Report for the National Commission on Excellence in Education.

ED 227 070. 59 pp. MF–01 PC–03.

———. 1984a. "Student Values: Knowing More About Where We Are Today." *AAHE Bulletin.* Washington, D.C.: American Association for Higher Education.

———. 1984b. "Student Involvement: A Developmental Theory for Higher Education." *Journal of College Student Personnel* 25(4): 297–308.

Astin, A. W.; Green, K. C.; Korn, W. S.; and Schalit, M. 1986. *The American Freshman: National Norms for Fall, 1986.* Los Angeles: Cooperative Institutional Research Program of the American Council on Education and University of California.

Astin, A. W.; Green, K. C.; and Korn, W. S. January 1987. *The American Freshman: Twenty Year Trends.* Los Angeles: Cooperative Institutional Research Program of the American Council on Education and University of California.

Astin, A. W., and Nichols, R. C. 1964. "Life Goals and Vocational Choice." *Journal of Applied Psychology* 48(1): 50–58.

Astin, A. W., and Panos, R. J. 1969. *The Educational and Vocational Development of College Students.* Washington, D.C.: American Council on Education.

Astin, A. W.; Panos, R. J.; and Creager, J. 1967. *National Norms for Entering College Freshmen Fall 1966.* Washington, D.C.: American Council on Education.

Augustin, J. W. 1985. "Adult Students and Career Planning." Research report. Green Bay: University of Wisconsin. ED 262 225. 48 pp. MF–01; PC–02.

Baer, M. L., and Carr, S. Summer 1985. "Academic Advisor: Catalyst for Achieving Institutional and Student Goals." *NASPA Journal* 23(1): 36–44.

Baird, L.L. November 1967. *The Undecided Student: How Different Is He?* ACT Research Report No. 22. Iowa City, Iowa: The American College Testing Program.

———. 1969. *Patterns of Educational Aspiration.* ACT Research Report No. 32. Iowa City, Iowa: The American College Testing Program.

———. n.d., circa 1986. "The Undergraduate Experience: Commonalities and Differences Among Colleges." Unpublished paper. Lexington: University of Kentucky.

Bandura, A. 1982. "Self-Efficacy Mechanism in Human Agency." *American Psychologist* 37(2): 122–48.

———. 1986. *Social Foundations of Thought and Action.* Englewood Cliffs, N.J.: Prentice-Hall.

Barrow, J. C. 1986. *Fostering Cognitive Development of Students.* San Francisco: Jossey-Bass.

Beal, P. E. July 1980. "Student Goals and Reasons for Attendance at a Denominational Institution." *Journal of College Student Per-*

sonnel 21(4): 312–19.

Bean, J. P. 1986. "The Clark-Trow Typology Revisited: Its Conceptual Validity and a Comparison of Threshold and Valence Theories in Explaining Students Outcomes from College." San Antoinio, Texas: Paper read at the Association for the Study of Higher Education, February.

Bers, T. H. 1986. "Confidence, Commitment, and Academic Performance and Retention of Community College Students." *Community/ Junior College Quarterly of Research and Practice* 10(1): 35–57.

Bloom, B. S., ed. 1956. *Taxonomy of Educational Objectives: Cognitive Domains.* New York: David McKay.

Boker, J. R., and Games, P. A. April 1980. "Effects of Motivational and Situational Variables on Achievement Performance." Boston: Paper read at the 64th annual meeting of the American Educational Research Association, April 7-11. Ed 189 119. 24 pp. MF–01; PC–01.

Bomotti, S. Smith. 1987. "Student Goals: A Literature Review." Ann Arbor: Unpublished paper submitted for research practicum, School of Education, University of Michigan, May.

Bowen, H. R. 1977. *Investment in Learning.* San Francisco: Jossey-Bass.

Bower, G. H. "Cognitive Psychology: An Introduction." In *Handbook of Learning and Cognitive Process,* vol. 1, edited by W. K. Estes. Hillsdale, N.J.: Lawrence Erlbaum Associates.

Boyer, E. L. 1987. *College: The Undergraduate Experience in America.* New York: Harper and Row.

Braskamp, L. A., and Maehr, M. 1988. *SPECTRUM: Assessment Surveys for Higher Education.* Champaign, Ill.: Metritech.

Brown, D. G. 1970. "A Scheme for Measuring the Output of Higher Education." In *Outputs of Higher Education: Their Identification, Measurement, and Evaluation,* edited by B. Lawrence, G. Weathersby, and V. W. Patterson, pp. 27–38. Boulder, Colo.: Western Interstate Commission for Higher Education.

Brown, D.; Brooks, L; et al. 1984. *Career Choice and Development.* San Francisco: Jossey-Bass.

Campbell, W. E., and Smith, M. P. 1985. *Current Student Survey Report.* Five parts. Rockville, Md.: Montgomery College, Office of Institutional Research.

Cantor, N.; Norem, J. K.; Niedenthal, P. M.; Langston, C. A.; and Brower, A. M. 1987. "Life Tasks, Self-Concept Ideals and Cognitive Strategies in a Life Transition." *Journal of Personality and Social Psychology* 53: 1178–91.

Capps, J. 1985. "Report on Evening Student Profile and Weekend College Survey, Spring Semester, 1985." Research report. Somerville, N.J.: Somerset Country College. ED 254 294. 31 pp. MF–01; PC–02.

Caracelli, V. J. April 1986. "The Career Goals of Reentry Women: A

Not So Hidden Agenda." San Francisco: Paper read at 70th annual meeting of the American Educational Research Association. ED 269 584. 40 pp. MF–01; PC–02.

Carmody, J. F.; Fenske, R. H.; and Scott, C. S. August 1972. *Changes in Goals, Plans and Background Characteristics of College-Bound High School Students.* ACT Research Report No. 54. Iowa City, Iowa: The American College Testing Program.

Centra, J. A. 1970. *The College Environment Revisited: Current Descriptions and a Comparison of Three Methods of Assessment.* RDR 70–71, No. 1, Research Bulletin RB 70–44. Princeton: Educational Testing Service.

Chickering, A. W. 1969. *Education and Identity.* San Francisco: Jossey-Bass.

———. 1974. *Commuting Vs. Resident Students: Overcoming the Educational Inequalities of Living Off Campus.* San Francisco: Jossey-Bass.

Chickering, A. W., et al. 1981. *he Modern American College.* San Francisco: Jossey-Bass.

Clark, B. R., and Trow, M. 1966. "The Organizational Context." In *College Peer Groups: Problems and Prospects for Research,* edited by T. M. Newcomb and

E. K. Wilson, pp. 17–70. Chicago: Aldine.

Claxton, C. S., and Murrell, P. H. 1987. *Learning Styles: Implications for Improving Education Practices.* ASHE-ERIC Higher Education No. 4, Washington, D.C.: Association for the Study of Higher Education. ED 293 478, 120 pp. MF–01; PC–05.

Cohen, A. M. 1986. "Perennial Issues in Community Colleges." Paper presented at seminar series. Raleigh: North Carolina State University. ED 270 139. 18 pp. MF–01; PC–01.

Cole, N. S., and Hanson, G. R. January 1971. *An Analysis of the Structure of Vocational Interests.* ACT Research Report No. 40. Iowa City, Iowa: The American College Testing Program.

Conrad, C., and Pratt, A. 1983. "Making Decisions About the Curriculum: From Metaphor to Model." *Journal of Higher Education* 54(1): 16–30.

Crites, John O. 1987. *Evaluation of Career Guidance Programs: Models, Methods, and Microcomputers.* Information Series No. 317. Research report. Columbus, Ohio: National Center for Research in Vocational Education, Ohio State University. ED 284 065. 37 pp. MF–01; PC–02.

Cross, K. P. 1986a. "Taking Teaching Seriously." Washington, D.C.: Paper presented at conference of American Association for Higher Education, March.

———. 1986b. "The Need for Classroom Research." Hidden Valley, Pa.: Paper presented at conference of Professional and Organizational Development Network in Higher Education, October 31.

———. 1988a. *Teaching Goals Inventory.* Cambridge: Harvard Graduate School of Education.

———. 1988b. "Feedback in the Classroom: Making Assessment Matter." Chicago: Paper presented at AAHE Assessment Forum, June 8-11.

Cross, K. P., and Angelo, T. A. 1988. *Classroom Assessment Techniques: A Handbook for Faculty.* Ann Arbor: University of Michigan, National Center for Research to Improve Postsecondary Teaching and Learning.

Daloz, L. A., and Pitkin, C. September 1976. "Standard Setting by Students and Community: How Much Is Enough?" CAEL Institutional Report, Community College of Vermont. Columbia, Md.: Cooperative Assessment of Experiential Learning. ED 148 852. 44 pp. MF–01; PC–02.

Davis, J. A. 1965. *Undergraduate Career Decisions.* Chicago: Aldine.

Davis, J. S., and Van Dusen, W. D. 1975. *A Survey of Student Values and Choices.* Atlanta: College Entrance Examination Board, Southern Regional Office.

Doan, H. M., and Verroye, P. 1985. *Retention/Attrition and Student Educational Objectives: NVCC Winter 1985 First Timers.* OIR Research Brief No. RB 85/86–07. Annandale.: Northern Virginia Community College. ED 271 142. 14 pp. MF–01; PC–01.

Dole, A., and Digman, J. 1967. "Factors in College Attendance." *Journal of Applied Psychology* 51(3): 247–53.

Donald, J. G. 1983. "Knowledge Structures: Methods for Exploring Course Content." *Journal of Higher Education* 54(1): 31–41.

Donald, J. G., and Sullivan, A. M., eds. 1985. "Using Research to Improve Teaching." New Directions for Teaching and Learning No. 23. San Francisco: Jossey-Bass.

Dressel, P. L., and Marcus, D. 1982. *On Teaching and Learning in College.* San Francisco: Jossey-Bass.

Dweck, C. S. 1985. "Intrinsic Motivation, Perceived Control, and Self-Evaluation Maintenance: An Achievement Goal Analysis." In *Research on Motivation in Education, Volume 2: The Classroom Milieu,* edited by R. Ames and C. Ames. New York: Academic Press.

Dweck, C. S., and Leggett, E. L. 1988. "A Social-Cognitive Approach to Motivation and Personality." *Psychological Review* 95(2): 256–73.

Earley, M.; Mentkowski, M.; and Schafer, J. 1980. *Valuing at Alverno: The Valuing Process in Liberal Education.* Milwaukee, Wis.: Alverno Products.

Educational Testing Service. 1971. *CSQ: Comparative Data.* Princeton: Institutional Research Program for Higher Education.

Eison, J. 1979. "A New Instrument for Assessing Students' Orientations Toward Grades and Learning." *Psychological Reports* 48: 919–24.

Eison, J.; Pollio, H.; and Milton, O. 1982. "Manual for Use with LOGO

II." Knoxville: The University of Tennessee, Learning Resource Center.

———. 1986. "Educational and Personal Characteristics of Four Different Types of Learning-and Grade-Oriented Students." *Contemporary Educational Psychology* 11(1): 54–67.

Elfner, E. S.; McLaughlin, R. K.; Williamsen, S. A.; and Hardy, R. R. 1985. "Assessing Goal-Related Student Outcomes for Academic Decision-Making." Portland, Ore.: Paper presented at annual forum of Association for Institutional Research, April 28-May 1. ED 259 669. 30 pp. MF–01; PC–02.

Erickson, S. C. 1974. *Motivation for Learning.* Ann Arbor: University of Michigan Press.

Ewell, P. T. 1983. *Student-Outcomes Questionnaires: An Implementation Handbook.* 2d ed. Boulder, Colo.: National Center for Higher Education Management Systems and The College Board.

Feldman, K. A., and Newcomb, T. M. 1969. *The Impact of College on Students.* San Francisco: Jossey-Bass.

Fenske, R., and Scott, C. 1973. "College Students' Goals, Plans, and Background Characteristics: A Synthesis of Three Empirical Studies." *Research in Higher Education* 1(2): 101–18.

Fleming, J. 1985. *Blacks in College.* San Francisco: Jossey-Bass.

Ford, M. E. 1986. "For All Practical Purposes: Criteria for Defining and Evaluating Practical Intelligence." In *Practical Intelligence,* edited by R. J. Sternberg and R. K. Wagner, pp. 183–200. New York: Cambridge University Press.

Fox, R. N. 1984. "Reliability and Discriminant Validity of Institutional Integration Scales for Disadvantaged College Students." *Educational and Psychological Measurement* 44(4): 1051–57.

Freeman, R. M., et al. 1986. "Surveying Student Goals to Aid Institutional Effectiveness: Student Goals Survey Research Report." Berkeley, Calif.: Vista College. ED 267 865. 18 pp. MF–01; PC–01.

Freeman, R., and Hollomon, J. H. September 1975. "The Declining Value of College Going." *Change* 7(7): 23–31.

Frewin, C. 1977. "The Relationship of Educational Goal-Setting Behavior to the Conceptual Level Model." Minneapolis: Paper presented at Adult Education Research conference, April.

Friedlander, J. 1982. "Measuring the Benefits of Liberal Arts Education in Washington's (State) Community Colleges." Research report. ED 217 918. 52 pp. MF–01; PC–03.

———. 1986. "A Follow-up Survey of Students Who Received a Degree or Certificate from Napa Valley (Calif.) College in the 1984-1985 Academic Year." Research Report. ED 269 118. 9 pp. MF–01; PC–01.

Friedlander, J.; and Gocke, S. 1985. "Results of the Fall, 1984 Survey of Napa Valley (Calif.) College Students." Research report. ED 256 427. 24 pp. MF–01; PC–01.

Fuchs, L., and Fuchs, D. 1985. "The Effect of Measuring Student Progress Toward Long- vs. Short-Term Goals: A Meta Analysis." Research report. Nashville, Tenn.: Vanderbilt University. ED 263 142. 27 pp. MF–01; PC–02.

Garland, H. 1983. "Influence on Ability, Assigned Goals, and Normative Information on Persons." *Journal of Applied Psychology* 983(68): 20–30.

Gell, R. L. July 1974. "Follow-up of Students Who Entered Montgomery Community College Fall 1970. A Preliminary Analysis of Student Goals." Research report. Rockville, Md.: Montgomery College, Office of Institutional Research. ED 097 053. 12 pp. MF–01; PC–01.

Gill, S. J., and Fruehling, J. A. July 1979. "Needs Assessment and the Design of Service Delivery Systems." *Journal of College Student Personnel* 20(4): 322–28.

Goldberg, A. S., and Shiflett, S. December 1981. "Goals of Male and Female College Students: Do Traditional Sex Differences Still Exist?" *Sex Roles: A Journal of Research* 7(12): 1213–22.

Gordon, V. N. 1984. *The Undecided College Student: An Academic and Career Advising Challenge.* Springfield, Ill.: Charles C. Thomas.

Gosman, E.; Dandridge, B.; Nettles, M.; and Thoeny, A. 1983. "Predicting Student Progression: The Influence of Race and Other Student Attributes and Institutional Characteristics on College Student Performance." *Research in Higher Education* 18(2): 209–36.

Green, K. C., and Astin, A. W. Winter 1985. "The Mood on Campus: More Conservative or Just More Materialistic?" *Educational Record* 66(1): 45–48.

Greenwood, G.; Hazelton, A.; Smith, A. B.; and Ware, W. B. 1976. "A Study of the Validity of Four Types of Student Ratings of College Teaching Assessed on a Criterion of Student Achievement Gains." *Research in Higher Education* 5(2): 171–78.

Hackman, J. R. 1983. "Designing Work for Individuals and Groups." In *Perspectives on Behavior in Organizations,* edited by J. R. Hackman, E. E. Lawler III, and L. W. Porter. New York: McGraw Hill.

Hackman, J. D., and Taber, T. D. Spring 1979. "Patterns of Undergraduate Performance Related to Success in College." *American Educational Research Journal* 16(2): 117–38.

Hanson, G. R. 1988. "Critical Issues in the Assessment of Value Added in Education." In *Implementing Outcomes Assessment: Promise and Perils,* edited by T. W. Banta. New Directions for Institutional Research No. 59, pp. 53–68. San Francisco: Jossey-Bass.

Hanson, G. R., and Cole, N. S. 1973. *The Vocational Interests of Young Adults.* Iowa City, Iowa: American College Testing Program.

Hawaii University. October 1980. "Results of the Fall 1980 Entering Student Survey. Student Flow Program, Report 7." Honolulu: Survey at Kapiolani Community College. ED 196 461. 40 pp. MF–01; PC–02.

Heist, P., ed. 1968. *The Creative College Student: An Unmet Challenge.*

San Francisco: Jossey-Bass.

Heist, P., and Yonge, G. 1968. *Omnibus Personality Inventory Manual (Form F)*. New York: The Psychological Corporation.

Holland, J. L. 1966. *The Psychology of Vocational Choice: A Theory of Personality Types and Model Environments*. Waltham, Mass.: Blaidsdell.

————. 1973. *Making Vocational Choices: A Theory of Careers*. Englewood Cliffs, N.J.: Prentice-Hall.

————. 1985. *Making Vocational Choices: A Theory of Vocational Personalities and Work Environments*. Englewood Cliffs, N.J.: Prentice-Hall.

Holland, J. L., and Whitney, D. R. April 1968. *Changes in the Vocational Plans of College Students: Orderly or Random?* ACT Research Report No. 25. Iowa City, Iowa: The American College Testing Program.

Houseworth, S., and Thirer, J. 1982. "Comparison of Motive to Succeed, Motive to Avoid Failure, and Fear of Success Levels Between Male and Female Intercollegiate Swimmers." Research report. Carbondale: Southern Illinois University. ED 244 916. 25 pp. MF–01; PC–02.

Huber, V. L. 1985. "Effects of Task Difficulty, Goal Setting, and Strategy on Performance of a Heuristic Task." *Journal of Applied Psychology* 70(3): 492–504.

Inglehart, M. R., et al. 1987. "The Impact of Possible Selves on Academic Achievement: A Longitudinal Analysis." Chicago: Paper presented at 59th annual meeting of Midwestern Psychological Association, May 7-9. ED 285 067. 17 pp. MF–01; PC–01.

Ivancevich, J. 1976. "Effects of Goal Setting on Performance and Job Satisfaction." *Journal of Applied Psychology* 61(5): 605–12.

Jackson, L. M., and Mather, D. 1985. "Reliability and Factorial Validity of the Student Development Inventory." *Educational and Psychological Measurement* 45(3): 671–77.

Jackson, S. E., and Zedeck, S. 1982. "Explaining Performance Variability: Contributions of Goal Setting, Task Characteristics, and Evaluative Contests." *Journal of Applied Psychology* 67: 759–68.

Jacobi, M.; Astin, A.; and Ayala, F. Jr. 1987. *College Student Outcomes Assessment: A Talent Development Perspective*. ASHE-ERIC Higher Education No. 7. Washington, D.C.: Association for the Study of Higher Education.

Katchadourian, H. A., and Boli, J. 1985. *Careerism and Intellectualism Among College Students*. San Francisco: Jossey-Bass.

Kees, D. J. 1962. "The Clark-Trow Typology Revisited." *Journal of College Student Personnel*. 15: 140–44.

Kees, D. J., and McDougall, W. P. May 1971. "A Validation Study of the Clark-Trow College Subculture Typology." *Journal of College Student Personnel* 12(3): 193–99.

Keniston, K. 1966. "The Faces in the Lecture Room." In *The Contemporary University: U.S.A.,* edited by R. S. Morrison. Boston: Houghton Mifflin Co.

King, P. M., and Fields, A. L. November 1980. "A Framework for Student Development: From Student Development Goals to Educational Opportunity Practice." *Journal of College Student Personnel* 21(6): 541–48.

Kinnick, M. K., Westine, J., and Kempner, K. 1987. "Beyond 'Front Door' Access: Attaining the Bachelor's Degree." Kansas City, Missouri: Paper presented at 27th annual forum of Association for Institutional Research, May 5.

Klinger, E. 1977. *Meaning and Void.* Minneapolis: University of Minnesota Press.

Koefoed, J. O., Jr. 1985. "An Examination of the Goals of Incoming Students at Kirkwood Community College." Research report. Kirkwood, Iowa. ED 262 848. 102 pp. MF–01; PC–05.

Kolb, D. A. 1976. *The Learning Styles Inventory: Technical Manual.* Boston: McBer.

———. 1981. "Learning Styles and Individual Differences." In *The Modern American College,* edited by A. W. Chickering. San Francisco: Jossey-Bass.

———. 1985. *The Learning Style Inventory.* Boston: McBer.

Krukowski, J. May/June 1985. "What Do Students Want? Status." *Change* 17(3): 21–28.

Lenning, O. T.; Lee, Y. S.; Micek, S. S.; and Service, A. L. 1977. *A Structure for the Outcomes of Postsecondary Education.* Boulder, Colo.: National Center for Higher Education Management Systems.

Lester, J. 1986. "Longitudinal Study of Freshmen Entering in 1982 in their Senior Year. Spring 1986." Research report. Notre Dame, Ind.: Saint Mary's College, April 4. ED 276 386. 27 pp. MF–01; PC–02.

Levin, B., and Clowes, D. January/March 1980. "Realization of Educational Aspirations Among Blacks and Whites at Two- and Four-Year Colleges." *Community/Junior College Research Quarterly* 4(2): 185–93.

Levine, A. 1981. *When Dreams and Heroes Died: A Portrait of Today's College Student.* San Francisco: Jossey-Bass.

———. April 1986. "Hearts and Minds: The Freshman Challenge." *AAHE Bulletin,* 3–6. ED 267 718. 5 pp. MF–01; PC–02.

Locke, E. A. 1967. "Motivational Effects of Knowledge of Results: Knowledge or Goal Setting." *Journal of Applied Psychology* 51: 324-39.

Locke, E. A.; Cartledge, N.; and Knerr, C. S. 1970. "Studies of Relationship Between Satisfaction, Goal-Setting, and Performance." *Organizational Behavior and Human Performance* 5: 135–58.

Locke, E. A.; Frederick, E.; Buckner, E.; and Bobko, P. 1984. "Effect of Previously Assigned Goals on Self-set Goals and Performance."

Journal of Applied Psychology 69(4): 694–99.

Locke, E. A.; Shaw, K. N.; Saari, L. M.; and Latham, G. P. 1981. "Goal Setting and Task Performance: 1969-1980." *Psychological Bulletin* 90(1): 125–52.

Longwood College. April 1986. "Longwood College Involvement Project." Farmville, Va: Paper from American Association for Higher Education Assessment Forum. ED 283 498. 38 pp. MF–01; PC–02.

Los Angeles Harbor College. 1982. "Student Objectives Survey." Research report. Wilmington, Calif. ED 138 320. 59 pp. MF–01; PC–03.

MacMillan, J. H. 1988. "Beyond Value-Added Education: Improvement Alone Is Not Enough." *Journal of Higher Education* 59(5): 564–79.

Maehr, M. L. 1984. "Meaning and Motivation: Toward a Theory of Personal Investment." In *Research on Motivation in Education,* vol. 1, *Student Motivation,* edited by R. Ames and C. Ames. New York: Academic Press.

Maehr, M. L., and Braskamp, L. A. 1986. *The Motivation Factor: A Theory of Personal Investment.* Lexington, Mass.: Lexington Books.

Manderlink, G., and Harackiewicz, J. M. 1984. "Proximal Versus Distal Goal Setting and Intrinsic Motivation." *Journal of Personality and Social Psychology* 47(4): 918–28.

Markus, H., and Wurf, E. 1987. "The Dynamic Self-Concept: A Social Psychological Perspective." In *Annual Review of Psychology,* vol. 38, edited by M. R. Rosenzweig and L. W. Porter. Palo Alto, Calif.: Annual Reviews.

Matsui, T.; Okada, A.; and Mizuguchi, R.D. 1981. "Expectancy Theory Prediction of the Goal Theory Postulate, 'The Harder the Goals the Higher the Performance.'" *Journal of Applied Psychology* 66(1): 54–62.

McClelland, D. C. 1965. "Toward a Theory of Motive Acquisition." *American Psychologist* 20: 321–33.

McCombs, B. L. 1984. "Processes and Skills Underlying Continuing Intrinsic Motivation to Learn: Toward a Definition of Motivational Skills Training Interventions." *Educational Psychologist* 19(4): 199–218.

McKeachie, W.; Pintrich, P.; Lin, Y.; and Smith, D. 1986. *Teaching and Learning in the College Classroom: A Review of the Research Literature.* Supplemented November 1987. Ann Arbor: University of Michigan, National Center for Research to Improve Postsecondary Teaching and Learning.

Mehrabian, A., and Bank, L. 1978. "A Questionnaire Measure of Individual Differences in Achieving Tendency." *Educational and Psychological Measurement* 38(2): 475–78.Mentkowski, M., and Loacker, G. 1985. "Assessing and Validating the Outcomes of College." In *Assessing Educational Outcomes,* edited by P. T. Ewell. New Directions for Institutional Research No. 47, pp. 47–64. San

Francisco: Jossey-Bass.

Milton, O.; Pollio, H.; and Eison, J. 1986. *Making Sense of College Grades.* San Francisco: Jossey-Bass.

Milwaukee Area Technical College. 1986. "Student Evaluation of the Milwaukee Area Technical College: 1986 Student Survey Report." Department of Research, Planning and Development. ED 272 261. 95 pp. MF–01; PC–04.

Moen, R., and Doyle, K. O., Jr. 1978. "Measures of Academic Motivation: A Conceptual Review." *Research in Higher Education* 8(1): 1–23.

Montemayor, J. J., et al. July 1985. "Glendale Community College Students' Educational Intent Survey, Spring 1985." Research Report 1. Arizona: Glendale Community College, Office of Research and Development. ED 281 572. 185 pp. MF–01; PC–08.

Morgan, M. 1981. "Self-Derived Objectives in Private Study." *Journal of Educational Research* 74(5): 327–32.

Morstain, B. R. 1973. *Student Orientations Survey: Form D, Preliminary Manual.* Newark: University of Delaware, Office of Academic Planning and Evaluation.

Moss, J. 1985. "SIQ—Student Information Questionnaire: A Survey of Student Characteristics, Fall 1984." San Francisco Community College District. ED 257 487. 673 pp. MF–04; PC–27.

National Center for Higher Education Management Systems and The College Board. 1983. *Student Outcomes Information Service.* Boulder, Colo.: National Center for Higher Education Management Systems.

National Institute of Education Study Group. 1984. *Involvement in Learning: Realizing the Potential of American Higher Education.* Washington, D.C.: U.S. Government Printing Office.

Neumann, L. 1982. "Goal Congruence and Instructional Satisfaction: A Comparison Among Three Academic Programs." *College Student Journal* 16(1): 38–44.

O'Connor, E. J., et al. December 1980. "Expended Effort and Academic Performance." *Teaching of Psychology* 7(4): 231–233.

Otto, A. M. 1980. "A Study to Determine Student Goals for Students Enrolled in a Community College." Research report. Florida Keys Community College. ED 191 521. 115 pp. MF–01; PC–05.

Pace, C. R. 1979a. *College Student Experiences.* Los Angeles: University of California, Graduate School of Education, Laboratory for Research on Higher Education.

———. 1979b. *Measuring Quality of Effort: A New Dimension for Understanding Student Learning and Development in College.* Los Angeles: University of California, Graduate School of Education, Laboratory for Research on Higher Education.

———. 1979c. "The Other Side of Accountability: Measuring Students' Use of Facilities and Opportunities." Paper presented at annual forum of Association for Institutional Research.

———. 1984. *Measuring the Quality of Student Experiences: An Account of the Development and Use of the College Student Experiences Questionnaire.* Los Angeles: University of California, Graduate School of Education, Higher Education Research Institute.

———. 1987. *CSEQ Test Manual Norms: College Student Experiences Questionnaire.* Los Angeles: University of California, Graduate School of Education, Center for the Study of Evaluation.

Pace, C. R., et al. 1975. *Higher Education Measurement and Evaluation Kit.* Los Angeles: University of California, Graduate School of Education, Laboratory for Research on Higher Education.

Pascarella, E. T. 1980. "Student-Faculty Informal Contact and College Outcomes." *Review of Educational Research* 50(4): 545–95.

———. 1985. "College Environmental Influences on Learning and Cognitive Development: A Critical Review and Synthesis." In *Higher Education: Handbook of Theory and Research,* vol. I, edited by J. M. Smart. New York: Agathon Press.

Pascarella, E. T., and Chapman, D. W. 1983. "Validation of a Theoretical Model of College Withdrawal: Interaction Effects in a Multi-institutional Sample." *Research in Higher Education* 19: 25–48.

Pascarella, E. T.; Duby, P. B.; and Iverson, B. K. 1983. "A Test and Reconceptualization of a Theoretical Model of College Withdrawal in a Commuter Institution Setting." *Sociology of Education* 56: 88–100.

Pascarella, E. T., and Terenzini, P. T. 1980. "Predicting Freshman Persistence and Voluntary Dropout Decisions from a Theoretical Model." *Journal of Higher Education* 51(1): 60–75.

Perry, W. G. 1970. *Forms of Intellectual and Ethical Development in the College Years: A Scheme.* New York: Holt, Rinehart and Winston.

———. 1981. "Cognitive and Ethical Growth: The Making of Meaning." In *The Modern American College,* edited by A. W. Chickering. San Francisco: Jossey-Bass.

Perry, R. P., and Dickens, W. J. 1987. "Perceived Control and Instruction in the College Classroom: Some Implications for Student Achievement." *Research in Higher Education* 27(4): 291–310.

Pervin, L. A., and Rubin, D. B. 1968. *Form A: An Instrument for the Measurement of Student Perceptions of College.* Research report. Princeton, N.J.

Peterson, M. W.; Blackburn, R. T.; Gamson, Z.; et al. 1978. *Black Students on White Campuses: The Impacts of Increased Black Enrollments.* Ann Arbor: University of Michigan, Institute for Social Research.

Peterson, R. E. 1971. "Intellectual Competence: Definition and Measurement." Research report. Princeton, N.J.: Educational Testing Service. ED 058 302. 12 pp. MF–01; PC–01.

Pintrich, P. R. 1988. "The Dynamic Interplay of Student Motivation
and Cognition in the College Classroom." In *Advances in Motivation and Achievement,* vol. 6, edited by M. Maehr and C. Ames.
Greenwich, Conn.: JAI Press.

Pintrich, P. R.; McKeachie, W. J.; Smith, D. A.; Doljanac, R.; Lin, Y.;
Naveh-Benjamin, M.; Crooks, T.; and Karabenick, S. 1988. *Motivated
Strategies for Learning Questionnaire (MSLQ).* Ann Arbor: University of Michigan, National Center for Research to Improve Postsecondary Teaching and Learning.

Pratt, A., and Conrad, C. 1981. "Everyman's Undergraduate Curriculum: A Question of Human Context." *Liberal Education* 67(2):
168–76.

Prediger, D. J.; Roth, J. D.; and Noeth, R. J. 1973. *Nationwide Study
of Student Career Development: Summary of Results.* ACT Research
Report No. 61. Iowa City, Iowa: The American College Testing
Program.

Quinley, J. W. 1983. "1978 Entrant Follow-up Study." Research report.
Bel Air, Md.: Harford Community College.
ED 231 432. 34 pp. MF–01; PC–02.

Reichel, A.; Newmann, Y.; and Pizam, A. 1981. "The Work Values and
Motivational Profiles of Vocational, Collegiate, Nonconformist,
and Academic Students." *Research in Higher Education* 14(3):
187–99.

Reichmann, S., and Grasha, A. 1974. "A Rational Approach to Developing and Assessing the Construct Validity of a Student Learning
Style Scales Instrument." *Journal of Psychology* 87: 213–23.

Rendon, L. 1983. "Chicano Students and Institution Related Deter-
minants of Educational Outcomes in South Texas Community College." New Orleans: Paper read at annual conference of American
Association of Community and Junior Colleges. ED 231 423. 33
pp. MF–01; PC–02.

Rice, R. 1983. "USC-Lancaster: A Follow-up Survey of Students at a
Two-Year Commuter Campus." Research report. Lancaster: University of South Carolina. ED 231 439. 12 pp. MF–01; PC–01.

Richards, J. M., Jr. 1966. "Life Goals of American College Freshmen."
Journal of Counseling Psychology 13(1): 12–20.

Richards, J. M., Jr.; Holland, J. L.; and Lutz, S. W. 1966a. *The Assessment
of Student Accomplishment in College.* ACT Research Report No.
11. Iowa City, Iowa: American College Testing Program.

———. 1966b. *The Prediction of Student Accomplishment in College.*
ACT Research Report No. 13. Iowa City, Iowa: American College
Testing Program.

Robbins, S. B., and Patton, M. J. 1985. "Self-Psychology and Career
Development: Construction of the Superiority and Goal Instability
Scales." *Journal of Counseling Psychology* 32(2): 221–31.

Rogers, A. 1986. *Teaching Adults.* Philadelphia: Open University Press.

Romano, R. 1985. "A Statistical Profile of the Entering Class at Broome Community College, Fall 1985: Student Characteristics, Needs, and Goals." Research report. Binghamton, N.Y. ED 263 972. 34 pp. MF–01; PC–02.

Rosenblurth, A. 1966. "Behavior, Purpose, and Teleology." In *Purpose in Nature*, edited by J. Feinberg and W. C. Salmon. Englewood Cliffs, N.J.: Prentice-Hall.

Rossmann, J., and El-Khawas, E. 1987. *Thinking About Assessment: Perspectives for Presidents and Chief Academic Officers.* Washington, D.C.: American Council on Education and American Association for Higher Education. ED 292 433. 28 pp. MF–01; PC–02.

Rush, I. E. 1983. "Comparative Study of Learning Styles and Related Factors Between Traditional and Nontraditional Students at the University of Akron." Detroit, Mich.: Paper presented at annual meeting of National Council on Aging, March 13-16. ED 240 408. 63 pp. MF–01; PC–03.

Sadler, D. R. 1983. "Evaluation and the Improvement of Academic Learning." *Journal of Higher Education* 54(1): 60–79.

Saunder, J., and Lancaster, G. 1980. "The Student Selection Process: A Model of Student Courses in Higher Education." Research report. Huddersfield Polytechnic, England. ED 207 402. 28 pp. MF–01; PC–02.

Schmeck, R.; Ribich, R.; and Ramanaiah, N. 1977. "Development of a Self-Report Inventory for Assessing Individual Differences in Learning Processes." *Applied Psychological Measurement* 1(3): 413–31.

Scott, K. J., and Robbins, S. B. March 1985. "Goal Instability: Implications for Academic Performance Among Students in Learning Skills Courses." *Journal of College Student Personnel* 26(2): 129–33.

Scott, T. B. 1980. "A Comparison of the Vocational Interest Profiles of Native American and Caucasian College-Bound Students." *Measurement and Evaluation in Guidance* 13(1): 35–42.

Shaw, K. M.; Stark, J. S.; Lowther, M. L.; and Wren, P. A. 1989. "Development of a Course-Specific Student Goals Instrument." Baltimore: Paper presented at Association of Institutional Research Forum.

Shearon, R. W. 1980. "Putting Learning to Work: A Profile of Students in North Carolina Community Colleges, Technical Institutes, and Technical Colleges. A Technical Report." Raleigh: North Carolina Community Colleges. ED 207 624. 266 pp. MF–01; PC–11.

Sheldon, M. S., and Grafton, C. L. November 1982. "Raison d'Etre: Students." *Community and Junior College Journal* 53(3): 19–20.

Showers, C., and Cantor, N. 1985. "Social Cognition: A Look at Motivational Strategies." In *Annual Review of Psychology,* edited by M. Rosenzweig and L. W. Porter, 36: 275–305. Palo Alto, Calif.: Annual Reviews.

Smart, J. C. 1985. "Holland Environments as Reinforcement Systems." *Research in Higher Education* 23(3): 279–92.

Stage, F. K. 1988. "Student Typologies and the Study of College Outcomes." *Review of Higher Education* 11(3): 247–57.

Stanton, C. 1978. "A Perception-Based Model for the Evaluation of Career and Value Education Within the Liberal Arts." *Journal of Higher Education* 49(1): 70–81.

Stark, J. S. 1975. "The Relation of Disparity in Student and Faculty Educational Attitudes to Early Student Transfer from College." *Research in Higher Education* 3(4): 329–44.

———. 1977. *The Many Faces of Educational Consumerism.* Lexington, Mass: D.C. Heath.

Stark, J. S.; Lowther, M. A.; and Hagerty, B. M. K. 1986. *Responsive Professional Education: Balancing Outcomes and Opportunities.* ASHE-ERIC Higher Education No. 3. Washington, D.C.: Association for the Study of Higher Education. ED 273 229. 127 pp. MF–01; PC–06.

Stark, J. S.; Lowther, M. A.; Ryan, M. P.; Bomotti, S. S.; Genthon, M.; Martens, G.; and Haven, C. L. 1988. *Reflections on Course Planning: Faculty and Students Consider Influences and Goals.* Ann Arbor: University of Michigan, National Center for Research to Improve Postsecondary Teaching and Learning.

Stark, J. S.; Lowther, M. A.; et al. In progress. 1989. *Technical Report of the Planning Introductory College Courses Study.* Ann Arbor: The University of Michigan, National Center for Research to Improve Postsecondary Teaching and Learning.

Stark, J. S., and Morstain, B. R. 1978. "Educational Orientations of Faculty in Liberal Arts Colleges: An Analysis of Disciplinary Differences." *Journal of Higher Education* 49(5): 420–37.

State University of New York at Plattsburgh. 1987. *Academic Development Survey.*

Stengel, B. S. 1981. "An Analysis of 'Student Outcomes.'" Paper presented at annual colloquium of Council of Graduate Students in Education. ED 221 498. 15 pp. MF–01; PC–01.

Stern, G. G. 1970. *People in Context: Measuring Person-Environment Congruence in Education and Industry.* New York: John Wiley and Sons.

Storr, A. 1961. *The Integrity of the Personality.* New York: Atheneum.

Super, D. E. 1970. *Work Values Inventory Manual.* Boston: Houghton Mifflin.

Super, D. E., et al, eds. 1963. *Career Development: Self-Concept Theory.* New York: College Entrance Examination Board.

Terborg, J. R. 1976. "The Motivational Components of Goal Setting." *Journal of Applied Psychology* 61(5): 613–21.

Terenzini, P. T. 1987. "A Review of Selected Theoretical Models of Student Development and Collegiate Impact." Paper presented at meeting of Association for the Study of Higher Education, Baltimore, Md., November.

Terenzini, P. T., et al. September/October 1984. "Influences on Students' Perceptions of Their Academic Skill Development During College." *Journal of Higher Education* 55(5): 621–36.

Terenzini, P. T., and Pascarella, E. T. 1977. "An Assessment of the Construct Validity of the Clark-Trow Typology of College Student Subcultures." *American Educational Research Journal* 14: 225–48.

Terenzini, P. T.; Pascarella, E. T.; and Lorang, W. G. 1982. "An Assessment of the Academic and Social Influences on Freshman Year Educational Outcomes." *Review of Higher Education* 5(2): 86–111.

Terenzini, P. T.; and Wright, T. M. 1987. "Influences on Students' Academic Growth During Four Years of College." *Research in Higher Education* 26(2): 161–79.

Theophilides, C.; Terenzini, P.; and Lorang, W. 1984. "Relation Between Freshman Year Experience and Perceived Importance of Four Major Educational Goals." *Research in Higher Education* 20(2): 235–52.

Thomas, C. R. 1984. "Regression of Myers-Briggs Type Scales." *Psychological Reports* 55: 568.

Thompson, B., and Rucker, R. 1980. "Two-Year College Students' Goals and Program Preferences." *Journal of College Student Personnel* 21(5): 393–98.

Thompson, K. S. 1981. "Changes in the Values and Lifestyle Preferences of University Students." *Journal of Higher Education* 52(5): 506–18.

Tiedeman, D. V., and O'Hara, R. P. 1963. *Career Development: Choice and Adjustment.* New York: College Entrance Examination Board.

Tinto, V. Winter 1975. "Dropout from Higher Education: A Theoretical Synthesis of Recent Research." *Review of Educational Research* 45(1): 89–125.

————. 1987. *Leaving College: Rethinking the Causes and Cures of Student Attrition.* Chicago: University of Chicago Press.

Tracey, T. J., and Sedlacek, W. E. 1987. "A Comparison of White and Black Student Academic Success Using Noncognitive Variables: A Lisrel Analysis." *Research in Higher Education* 27(4): 333–48.

Walleri, R. D., and Peglow-Hoch, M. 1988. "Case Studies of Nontraditional High Risk Students: Does Social and Academic Integration Apply?" Paper presented at 28th annual forum of Association for Institutional Research, Phoenix, Ariz.: May 15-18.

Walsh, W. B. 1973. *Theories of Person-Environment Interaction: Implications for the College Student.* Iowa City, Iowa: American College Testing Program.

Ward, C. H. 1985. "Type A Performance Standards and Goal Achievement." Los Angeles: Paper presented at 93rd annual convention of American Psychological Association, August 23-27. ED 262 303. 31 pp. MF–01; PC–02.

Ward, T. J., Jr., and Clark, H. T., III. 1987. "The Effect of Field Dependence and Outline Condition on Learning High- and Low-Structure Information from a Lecture." *Research in Higher Education* 27(3): 259–72.

Weiner, B. 1985. *Human Motivation.* New York: Springer-Verlag.

———. 1986. *An Attributional Theory of Motivation and Emotion.* New York: Springer-Verlag.

Weiner, B.; Russell, D.; and Lerman, D. 1972. "The Cognition-Emotion Process in Achievement-Related Contexts." *Journal of Personality and Social Psychology* 37: 1211–20.

Weissberg, M.; Berentsen, M.; Cote, A.; Cravey, B.; and Heath, K. March 1982. "An Assessment of the Personal, Career, and Academic Needs of Undergraduate Students." *Journal of College Student Personnel* 23(2): 115–22.

Wicker, F. W.; Lambert, F. B.; Richardson, F. C.; and Kahler, J. 1984. "Categorical Goal Hierarchies and Classification of Human Motives." *Journal of Personality* 52(3): 285–305.

Wilder, M. A., Jr., and Kellams, S. E. 1987. "Commitment to College and Student Involvement." Washington, D.C.: Paper presented at meeting of American Educational Research Association, April.

Williams, E. P., and Williamson, M. M. 1985. "Characteristics of Students and Programs at Portland Community College." Research report. Portland, Oreg. ED 267 842. 54 pp. MF–01; PC–03.

Willingham, W. W. 1985. *Success in College: The Role of Personal Qualities and Academic Ability.* New York: College Entrance Examination Board.

Wilson, R. C.; Gaff, J. G.; Dienst, E. R.; Wood, L.; and Bavry, J. L. 1975. *The Impact of College on Students.* New York: John Wiley and Sons.

Witkin, H. A.; Moore, C. A.; Goodenough, D. R.; and Cox, P. W. 1977. "Field-Dependent and Field-Independent Cognitive Styles and Their Educational Implications." *Review of Educational Research* 47: 1–64.

Wittrock, M. C. 1986. "Student Thought Processes." In *Handbook of Research on Teaching,* edited by M. C. Wittrock. New York: Macmillan.

Wright, T. 1982. "Student Reaction to College." Research Report No. 82-09. Miami, Florida: Miami-Dade Community College. ED 226 781. 50 pp. MF–01; PC–03.

INDEX

A

AAC (see Association of American Colleges)
AASCU (see American Association of State Colleges and Universities)
Academic goals, 18
Academic integration, 55–56
Acceptance of goals, 40
Accommodators (learning style), 53
Achievement: classroom assessment, 3
ACT (see American College Testing program)
Active learning, 51
Administrative planning, 5, 74–75
Adult students, 7, 16, 57
Advising (see also Counseling improvement), 7
Affective factors, 44
African-American, 29, 58
Alumni surveys, 13
Alverno College, 8, 26
American Association of State Colleges and Universities (AASCU), 7
American College Testing program (ACT), 63
American College Testing Service, 69
Aptitude tests, 40, 63
Articulation of goals, 20–21
Assessment
       classroom achievement, 3
       course-level efforts, 60–61
       goal changes, 4, 60
       goals inventory use, 73–75
       outcomes, 2–3
       program requirements, 9
Assigned goals, 39, 40
Assimilators (learning style), 53
Association of American Colleges (AAC), 7
Astin-Panos-Creager typology, 26
Attributes of goals, 33–34
Attribution theory, 50–51
Attrition theory, 55, 77

B

Basic skills, 13

C

Career choice, 12, 17, 29, 35, 68
Careerists, 29
Carnegie Foundation for the Advancement of Teaching, 7
Causality, 50
Challenge of goals, 36–37

Student Goals in College and Courses

college, 1, 3
educational, 8
Models
intellectual growth, 65–67
learner development, 69
multidimensional, 70–71
personal/social development, 67
vocational development, 68–69
Motivated Strategies for Learning Questionnaire (MSLQ), 39, 48
Motivation, 5–6, 34, 39, 45, 46–49
MSLQ (see Motivated Strategies for Learning Questionnaire)
Multidimensional goals inventory model, 70
Myers-Briggs Type Indicator, 52

N

National Center for Research to Improve Postsecondary Teaching
and Learning (NCRIPTAL), 26
National Institute of Education (NIE), 6
National reports, 6–7
NCRIPTAL (see National Center for Research to Improve
Postsecondary Teaching and Learning)
NIE (see National Institute of Education)
Nondirectedness, 40

O

Omnibus Personality Inventory, 23
Orientation: exploratory/preparatory, 28
Outcomes
assessment, 2–3, 12, 30
link with goals, 35
student/course goals, 61
Ownership of goals, 39–40

P

Patterns of goals, 61, 63
Perry developmental theory, 54, 66
Personal goals, 15, 16, 35, 67, 76
Personality
theory, 27, 51, 53
types, 22, 29
Pintrich questionnaire, 52, 63, 69
Planning: data collection, 5
Productivity, 40

Q

Quality of effort, 57–58, 63
Questionnaires, 13, 22, 23, 26, 39, 48, 52, 63, 69

ASHE-ERIC HIGHER EDUCATION REPORTS

Since 1983, the Association for the Study of Higher Education (ASHE) and the Educational Resources Information Center (ERIC) Clearinghouse on Higher Education, a sponsored project of the School of Education and Human Development at The George Washington University, have cosponsored the *ASHE-ERIC Higher Education Report* series. The 1989 series is the eighteenth overall and the first to be published by the School of Education and Human Development at the George Washington University.

Each monograph is the definitive analysis of a tough higher education problem, based on thorough research of pertinent literature and insitutional experiences. Topics are identified by a national survey. Noted practitioners and scholars are then commissioned to write the reports, with experts providing critical reviews of each manuscript before publication.

Eight monographs (10 before 1985) in the ASHE-ERIC Higher Education Report series are published each year and are available on a individual or subscription basis. Subscription to eight issues is $80.00 annually; $60 to members of AAHE, AIR, or AERA; and $50 to ASHE members. All foreign subscribers must include an additional $10 per series year for postage.

Prices for single copies, including book rate postage, are $15.00 regular and $11.25 for members of AERA, AIR, AAHE, and ASHE ($10.00 regular and $7.50 for members for 1985 to 1987 reports, $7.50 regular and $6.00 for members for 1983 and 1984 reports, $6.50 regular and $5.00 for members for reports published before 1982). All foreign orders must include $1.00 per book for foreign postage. Fast United Parcel Service or first class postage is available for $1.00 per book in the U.S. and $2.50 per book outside the U.S. (orders above $50.00 may substitute 5% of the total invoice amount for domestic postage). Make checks payable to ASHE-ERIC. For VISA and MasterCard payments, include card number, expiration date, and signature. Orders under $25 must be prepaid. Bulk discounts are available on orders of 15 or more reports (not applicable to subscription orders). Order from the Publications Department, ASHE-ERIC Higher Education Reports, The George Washington University, One Dupont Circle, Suite 630, Washington, DC 20036-1183, or phone us at (202) 296-2597. Write for a complete catalog of all available reports.

1989 ASHE-ERIC Higher Education Reports

1. Making Sense of Administrative Leadership: The 'L' Word in Higher Education
   Estela M. Bensimon, Anna Neumann, and Robert Birnbaum

2. Affirmative Rhetoric, Negative Action: African-American and Hispanic Faculty at Predominantly White Universities
   Valora Washington and William Harvey

---

2. Working Effectively with Trustees: Building Cooperative Campus Leadership
   Barbara E. Taylor

3. Formal Recognition of Employer-Sponsored Instruction: Conflict and Collegiality in Postsecondary Education
   Nancy S. Nash and Elizabeth M. Hawthorne

4. Learning Styles: Implications for Improving Educational Practices
   Charles S. Claxton and Patricia H. Murrell

5. Higher Education Leadership: Enhancing Skills through Professional Development Programs
   Sharon A. McDade

6. Higher Education and the Public Trust: Improving Stature in Colleges and Universities
   Richard L. Alfred and Julie Weissman

7. College Student Outcomes Assessment: A Talent Development Perspective
   Maryann Jacobi, Alexander Astin, and Frank Ayala, Jr.

8. Opportunity from Strength: Strategic Planning Clarified with Case Examples
   Robert G. Cope

1986 ASHE-ERIC Higher Education Reports

1. Post-tenure Faculty Evaluation: Threat or Opportunity?
   Christine M. Licata

2. Blue Ribbon Commissions and Higher Education: Changing Academe from the Outside
   Janet R. Johnson and Laurence R. Marcus

3. Responsive Professional Education: Balancing Outcomes and Opportunities
   Joan S. Stark, Malcolm A. Lowther, and Bonnie M.K. Hagerty

4. Increasing Students' Learning: A Faculty Guide to Reducing Stress among Students
   Neal A. Whitman, David C. Spendlove, and Claire H. Clark

5. Student Financial Aid and Women: Equity Dilemma?
   Mary Moran

6. The Master's Degree: Tradition, Diversity, Innovation
   Judith S. Glazer

7. The College, the Constitution, and the Consumer Student: Implications for Policy and Practice
   Robert M. Hendrickson and Annette Gibbs

8. Selecting College and University Personnel: The Quest and the Question
   Richard A. Kaplowitz

1985 ASHE-ERIC Higher Education Reports

1. Flexibility in Academic Staffing: Effective Policies and Practices
   Kenneth P. Mortimer, Marque Bagshaw, and Andrew T. Masland

2. Associations in Action: The Washington, D.C. Higher Education Community
   Harland G. Bloland

3. And on the Seventh Day: Faculty Consulting and Supplemental Income
   Carol M. Boyer and Darrell R. Lewis

4. Faculty Research Performance: Lessons from the Sciences and Social Sciences
   John W. Creswell

5. Academic Program Review: Institutional Approaches, Expectations, and Controversies
   Clifton F. Conrad and Richard F. Wilson

6. Students in Urban Settings: Achieving the Baccalaureate Degree
   Richard C. Richardson, Jr. and Louis W. Bender

7. Serving More Than Students: A Critical Need for College Student Personnel Services
   Peter H. Garland

8. Faculty Participation in Decision Making: Necessity or Luxury?
   Carol E. Floyd

1984 ASHE-ERIC Higher Education Reports

1. Adult Learning: State Policies and Institutional Practices
   K. Patricia Cross and Anne-Marie McCartan

2. Student Stress: Effects and Solutions
   Neal A. Whitman, David C. Spendlove, and Claire H. Clark

3. Part-time Faulty: Higher Education at a Crossroads
   Judith M. Gappa

4. Sex Discrimination Law in Higher Education: The Lessons of the Past Decade
   J. Ralph Lindgren, Patti T. Ota, Perry A. Zirkel, and Nan Van Gieson

5. Faculty Freedoms and Institutional Accountability: Interactions and Conflicts
   Steven G. Olswang and Barbara A. Lee

6. The High Technology Connection: Academic/Industrial Cooperation for Economic Growth
   Lynn G. Johnson

7. Employee Educational Programs: Implications for Industry and Higher Education
   Suzanne W. Morse

8. Academic Libraries: The Changing Knowledge Centers of Colleges and Universities
   Barbara B. Moran

9. Futures Research and the Strategic Planning Process: Implications for Higher Education
   James L. Morrison, William L. Renfro, and Wayne I. Boucher

10. Faculty Workload: Research, Theory, and Interpretation
    Harold E. Yuker

1983 ASHE-ERIC Higher Education Reports

1. The Path to Excellence: Quality Assurance in Higher Education
   Laurence R. Marcus, Anita O. Leone, and Edward D. Goldberg

2. Faculty Recruitment, Retention, and Fair Employment: Obligations and Opportunities
   John S. Waggaman

3. Meeting the Challenges: Developing Faculty Careers*
   Michael C.T. Brooks and Katherine L. German

4. Raising Academic Standards: A Guide to Learning Improvement
   Ruth Talbott Keimig

5. Serving Learners at a Distance: A Guide to Program Practices
   Charles E. Feasley

6. Competence, Admissions, and Articulation: Returning to the Basics in Higher Education
   Jean L. Preer

7. Public Service in Higher Education: Practices and Priorities
   Patricia H. Crosson

8. Academic Employment and Retrenchment: Judicial Review and Administrative Action
   Robert M. Hendrickson and Barbara A. Lee

9. Burnout: The New Academic Disease*
   Winifred Albizu Melendez and Rafael M. de Guzmán

10. Academic Workplace: New Demands, Heightened Tensions
    Ann E. Austin and Zelda F. Gamson

*Out-of-print. Available through EDRS. Call 1-800-227-ERIC.

ORDER FORM

SAN DIEGO

Quantity   **Amount**

_____ Please begin my subscription to the 1989 *ASHE-ERIC Higher Education Reports* at $80.00, 33% off the cover price, starting with Report 1, 1989   _____

_____ Please begin my subscription to the 1990 *ASHE-ERIC Higher Education Reports* at $80.00 starting with Report 1, 1990   _____

_____ Outside the U.S., add $10 per series for postage   _____

Individual reports are avilable at the following prices:

1988 and forward, $15	1983 and 1984, $7.50
1985 to 1987, $10	1982 and back, $6.50

Book rate postage within the U.S. is included. Outside U.S., please add $1 per book for postage. Fast U.P.S. shipping is available within the U.S. at $1 per book; outside the U.S., $2.50 per book; orders over $50 may add 5% of the invoice total. All orders under $25 must be prepaid.

PLEASE SEND ME THE FOLLOWING REPORTS:

Quantity	Report No.	Year	Title	Amount

Subtotal:	
Postage (optional):	
Total Due:	

Please check one of the following:
- ☐ Check enclosed, payable to GWU-ERIC.
- ☐ Purchase order attached.
- ☐ Charge my credit card indicated below:
- ☐ Visa   ☐ MasterCard

Expiration Date _____

Name _____

Title _____

Institution _____

Address _____

City _____ State _____ Zip _____

Phone _____

Signature _____

SEND ALL ORDERS TO:
ASHE-ERIC Higher Education Reports
The George Washington University
One Dupont Circle, Suite 630
Washington, DC 20036-1183
Phone: (202) 296-2597